CONFESSIONS OF A VERMONT REALTOR ®

(an optimistic retrospective)

*9/10/94
To John McVicar
who can relate
to these tales.
Best wishes,
Bob*

By Robert P. Murray

Acknowlegdements

My thanks for the expertise and encouragement of Richard Abbott of Montreal and Susan Gregory Heaps of Westford, Vermont.
Also thanks to Jules Coxhill of South Africa for creating the fine sketches while her broken leg was healing. . .
and the many others who refused to let me give up.

I also want to cite the creative photography of:
— David Brownell for the cover
— Michael Clark for location shots
— The Stowe Reporter for photos loaned from their archives
— Jim Mitchell for his scintillating mural of the "Reluctant Panther"

® Realtor is the registered trademark which identifies a professional in Real estate who is a member of the National Association of Realtors.

TABLE OF CONTENTS

Introduction: Genesis 1
Prologue: Definitions 5
1. How I Bought My Farm and Happened into a Real Estate Career 12
2. Kirby 22
3. "The Reluctant Panther" 32
4. The Post-Graduate Paper Chase 40
5. "The Prince and the Pauper" 51
6. Being in the Right Place at the Right Time or Sometimes it's not what you know, but who you know 56
7. "The Lord Giveth and the Lord Taketh Away" 60
8. From the Pages of Horatio Alger 67
9. "It's an Ill Wind that Blows No One Some Good" 78
10. Trust, What a Wonderful Word! 85
11. "Now Who's Crazy?" 91
12. "A Nest of Robins in Its Hair" 98
13. Them and Us 106
14. A Tough New York Female 114
15. Development on a Micro-Scale 119

TABLE OF CONTENTS (Cont.)

16. Rights of Way 129
17. Ineptitude 134
18. The Redcoats are Coming ... The Redcoats
    are Coming 143
19. The Duke of Aragon 152
20. Selling the Sizzle 160
21. Aqua Pure "As Long as Grass Shall Grow or
    Waters Flow" 165
22. "Hanging in There" or
    "It Ain't Over 'til the Fat Lady Sings" 177
23. The High Wire Act 186
24. The Sign 195
25. "Wrap It Up, I'll Take It!" 200
26. Poetic Justice 205
27. Ditties 211
28. Vignettes 223
29. When is Enough 236

Introduction

Genesis

When I was a teenager, growing up in the affluent commuter suburb of Larchmont, New York, my family had a close friend in the real estate business. Watching her operate, I decided that real estate had to be the easiest way ever devised to make a handsome living. You apparently escorted people around to see some lovely homes; they chose the one they liked best; you drew up an amicable agreement of sale; and a couple of weeks later, after the lawyers and bankers completed their work, you attended a closing to pick up your, unconscionably-large, commission check.

Dream on, sweet bird of youth! When the average person, no matter how wealthy, lays down a substantial portion of his life savings to acquire one of the most valuable assets of another, then it's better than even money that tension and complications will ensue.

After those naive, younger years of school, sports, and the good life in Larchmont, I went on to Cornell University where I applied myself with greater abandon to ice hockey than to academics. But after the Navy had

INTRODUCTION

borrowed me for a couple of years, I returned to graduate from the University of Pennsylvania's Wharton School of Finance, equipped to face the world of business.

To the consternation of my family and friends, however, I then took a year's detour to try my hand as a radio host and entertainer in New Haven. When this turned out to be great food for the ego but not for the pocketbook, I finally succumbed to practicality and synthesized all this diverse training into a 12-year career in the radio and television business on Madison Avenue in New York.

New York television was fascinating and I enjoyed a great degree of success and status therein, but eventually the pleasures and pressures of that high-intensity business, combined with the sideline of playing guitar at parties and clubs, took its toll on my health and psyche. I experienced what could loosely be called a nervous breakdown. I found myself withdrawing more and more and ceasing to function effectively in either my business or my social life. It became apparent that at age 31 I had to withdraw from the urban rat race even if it was to be at great financial sacrifice.

In contemplating my escape, I kept remembering my old skiing mecca of Stowe, Vermont. I concluded that God, and my need for a little more serenity, were pointing me in that direction, so back-to-the-wall, I gathered my meager savings, my meager possessions, my guitar, and my skis and headed for Vermont.

Fortunately for this transition, during one vacation I had sung for the women who owned the Baggie Knee's, Stowe's only nightclub at the time. Nancy and Marie had cleverly converted Mrs. Moriarity's barn into an ultimately rustic nightclub. They were happy to hire me as a roving singer of folk songs, as I must have broken all records for minimum entertainment wages. Whether I was good or not, I sure-as-hell was a bargain, and in the process of working as an entertainer I got to know and be known by a wide cross-section of the eastern skiing world.

Eventually, Don Boardman at the Topnotch lured me away to be a combination singer/bartender at his lodge. There I found myself busy with enough menial activity to give my nerves and neuroses time to settle down, buoyed up by the immediate gratification of tips and applause.

Two years later, I had just bought an 1825 farmhouse and 65 acres for $7,000 (even then an amazing bargain), when I made my first trip back to Larchmont to attend the wedding of an old pal at the Larchmont Yacht Club: a milieu, I hasten to add, which had already become very foreign to my new economic impoverishment.

In relating the story of my wonderful farmhouse purchase (with my last $3,000 in cash and a $4,000 bank loan), I elicited the repeated request that I find something of the same description for my affluent former cohorts. So right then and there I thought, "I'll go back to Vermont, get my real estate license, and make the odd casual sale, which will greatly enhance my bartending income." You see, I still had the idealized image of real estate that had been implanted in my mind as a teenager.

Now don't get me wrong, real estate for the past 28

INTRODUCTION

years has been a fascinating adventure. I've prospered, stayed miraculously free of recrimination and lawsuits, and have gotten to know and enjoy an incredible variety of humanity and human motivation. I've been alternatively disappointed by people's avarice and greed, and then had my faith restored by stunning generosity. I told a minister one day that if he really wanted to relate to the vicissitudes of the Hebrews and the parables of the New Testament, he should take a couple of years off and sell real estate . . . "that's where the moral rubber meets the road," I told him . . . I don't think he got what I was talking about.

I'm sure, over the years, I've bent many of the rules of my so-called profession, but my simple guiding tenets have been: 1) to try to learn and fulfill the aspirations and needs of customers and clients; 2) to be as painfully honest as possible while trying to arbitrate between sometimes adversarial principals; 3) to facilitate the transaction with every fiber of my body, down to mowing lawns or carrying survey poles, and 4) to make my commission a secondary consideration which will come if all the other things happen and providence smiles on the deal.

In this treatise, I want to relate some of the very human and oft hilarious episodes that have befallen the plying of my trade. The tales may sound embellished, but they are all true and only a few names have been changed to protect the innocent . . . or the guilty . . . and to keep me out of court.

PROLOGUE

Definitions

When I started in real estate in 1963, much of Vermont was still available at about $150 an acre. That's 208 ft. x 208 ft. (almost the size of a football field) in perpetuity, all the way down to China, with annual taxes as low as $1.50 per acre. At the time, neither the big developers nor the environmentalists had arrived in Vermont to tempt us or save us from ourselves, so real estate was pretty darn laissez-faire. In the ensuing 30 years, the value of real estate has grown exponentially, but so has the interest on bank loans, property tax rates, and a phalanx of environmental regulations that would confound a dedicated Washington bureaucrat.

Meanwhile, the real estate business itself has greatly increased in sophistication with multiple listing systems, computerized marketing, and a new emphasis on protection from liability in this litigious age when clients may sue at the drop of a hat. But communication, honesty, and hard, tenacious work still prevail, and real estate can still be a challenging and rewarding adventure.

CONFESSIONS OF A VERMONT REALTOR

PROLOGUE

Before I get into the lighter side of my story, and its' hopefully humorous anecdotes let me digress for a moment while I try to define the real estate process. Corny as it may sound, real estate is, in many ways, a microcosm of life. The thirst for ownership of land, for instance, reflects an elemental human instinct deep in our ancestral genes.

That ancient hunger for the ownership of real estate still pervades much of the world, and the absence of private ownership even seems to have stifled productivity in the communist world. We Americans have enjoyed the greatest percentage of private home ownership in the world and each of us can at least cherish the hope of owning our own house or land.

That ownership ranges from the thousand-acre spread of the mid-west wheat farmer to the New York urbanite who identifies with a couple of dearly purchased, arms-length acres in Vermont. In the process of this acquisition of real estate, the broker really acts as a facilitator or arbiter trying to achieve a willing buyer, a willing seller, and a satisfied meeting of minds and purposes: a deal where both parties to a transaction go away feeling they prevailed, achieved their goals, made the proverbial good deal or a least a fair one. By law in Vermont, a broker must represent either buyer or seller, not both. But in reality he is usually trying to arrive at a fair exchange of values.

There are many kinds of real estate salespeople and brokers. For instance, there is the prime mover, dominant personality with a drive to steer and influence his customers; to maneuver the buyer and seller into responding to the broker's will. Then there is the high pressure salesperson, who may try to convince a prospect that this property is a steal that must be acted upon "now" because of the competitive buyers waiting in the wings.

But I think the preponderance of Real estate brokers truly want to read your dreams and desires and then fulfill them to the best of their ability. I really believe that, with most brokers, the commission is a secondary consideration to trying to fulfill and fortify the seller's or buyer's valid decision.

Except for those rare individuals with ultimate self-confidence, all buyers and sellers reach a critical moment in a deal when they question their own judgment . . . at that moment, they need fortification and reassurance from their agent. A good agent supplies that from sincerity, or on the other hand, is ready to dissuade a client or customer from an ill-advised transaction. That's not only good ethics, but it's also good business, because real estate is rarely a one- shot involvement, and the people to whom or for whom we sell in our community are wont to be our friends and neighbors into the future.

Of course, bringing a willing seller and a willing buyer together may be only 33% of the broker's involvement. Between contract and final closing may lie a minefield of zoning regulations, infirmities and flaws in the title, mortgage banking hurdles, road access problems . . . all the way to a possible bounced check at the closing. As Yogi Berra says, "It ain't over til it's over," and a good agent needs patience, staying power, and the ability to reassure waning parties who become temporarily disaffected.

PROLOGUE

But perhaps the most vital lesson for any prospective real estate broker to learn is never to "cry over spilt milk." If you've worked assiduously for six months on a deal and it falls apart at the last minute, and then the prospect adds insult to injury by buying a major property through a competitor . . . "pick yourself up, brush yourself off, and start all over again." In real estate, as in life, if you're looking for justice you're destined to be sorely disappointed. There are some wonderful unexpected rewards, but there's no immediate correlation between effort and fruition. So persevere, dwell on the good things, and don't allow yourself to be sidetracked by dwelling on life's injustices. That's a plentiful waste of time.

Also, the broker had better be prepared to meet with so-called 'good friends' who will, opportunistically, drop him or her like a hot potato, and others whose loyalty and appreciation will bring tears to ones eyes. And for yourself, don't miss those chances to be generous in dividing a commission among co-brokers; nor to thank someone for their help or a job well done; nor to be really honest in a deal, even at the cost of a short-term advantage. Because, over a period of years, honesty, generosity, fairness, hard work are the practices that pay off in success, gratification, and lasting friendships through real estate. Nice guys do finish first. Leo Durocher was not a Realtor.

Now, having stated all these pseudo-profound axioms, let me add that in experiencing the "slings and arrows of outrageous fortune" of this profession, I have also thoroughly enjoyed the whimsical events reflective of the foibles of human nature . . . and the darndest twists of so-called sane-minded people abetted by my own ineptitude. My career often reads like a Laurel and Hardy script, but I hope you'll find it a cross-section of the occurrences that have befallen all of us who have ever bought a home, owned land, or rented an apartment.

This series of episodes grew out of my life as a country Realtor for close to 30 years. *The anecdotes and essays that follow are not arranged in any particular order. You can read them in sequence or dip in and out as your interests dictate.* Either way, I hope you will enjoy this one man's odyssey.

And so, I give you "Confessions of a Vermont Realtor."

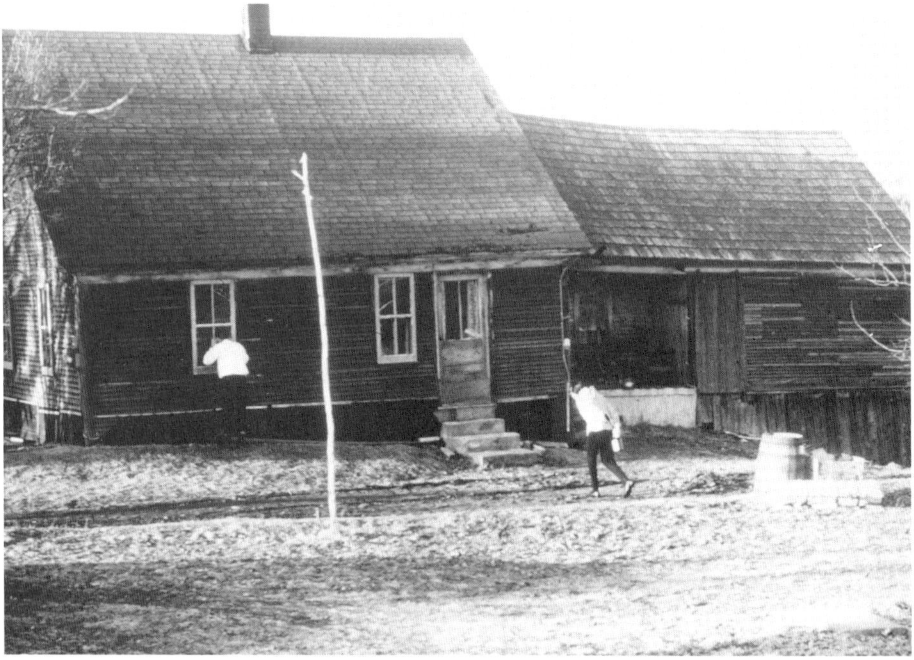

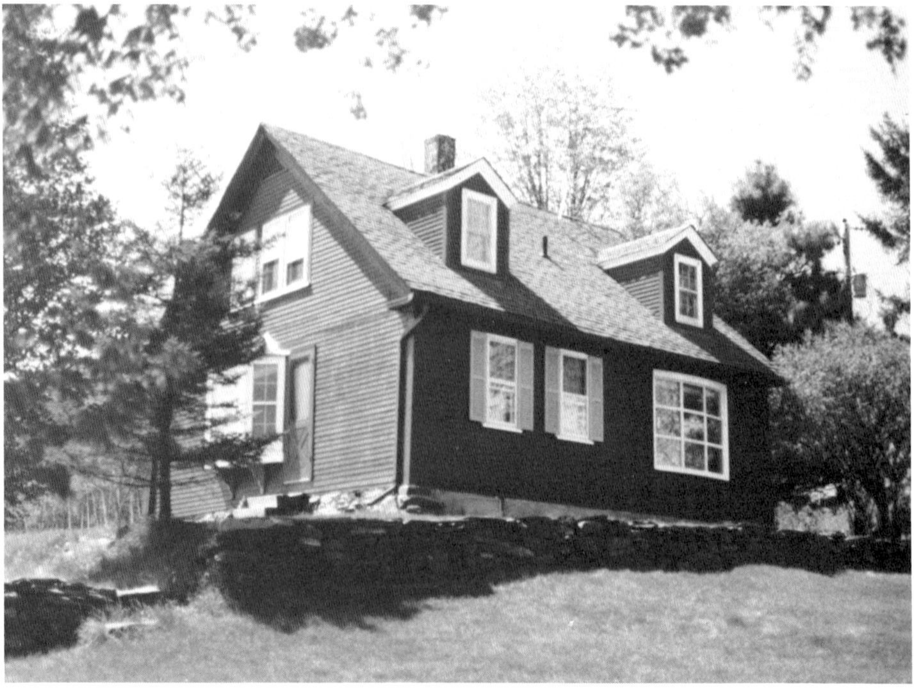

*How I Bought My Farm and
Happened into a
Real Estate Career*

Chapter 1

As you've learned from the introduction, I escaped to Vermont in 1963, a casualty of working and playing too feverishly in New York's radio and TV business.

Arriving in Stowe, virtually broke and broken, I eked out a subsistence playing guitar and tending bar. Bartending required very little worry, planning, or emotional involvement, so it was great therapy at just the time in my life when I needed it.

Then, one fortuitous night late that year, a fun-loving group of young people from Montreal dropped into the Topnotch Bar where I was working. After filling their glasses, I took up my guitar and regaled my captive audience with folk songs and ditties. They responded with applause and invited me out the next day to share brunch and help them "lay roof" on their farmhouse addition on Gregg Hill.

I turned to the most striking of the young women to ask if she would be "laying roof tomorrow," and without batting an eye she replied, "I'm not laying anyone tomorrow." Now a comment like that does tend to arouse one's

HOW I BOUGHT MY FARM AND HAPPENED INTO A REAL ESTATE CAREER

curiosity, so next morning I showed up at the chalet site, hammer in hand.

However, once on the roof of the chalet, I quickly became more enthralled with the magnificently contoured natural beauty of Waterbury Center's farmland than I was with the contours of the young woman of the previous evening. I therefore said to Phil, the Canadian owner of this beautiful spread, "Won't you sell me a few acres of your obvious abundance of land?"

"Not a square foot," he replied, "but the farmer across the road wants to sell his dilapidated farmhouse and 65 acres for $7,500."

Without hesitation, I clambered down from the roof, took myself across the road, and knocked on the door of an incredibly decrepit, albeit classic Vermont farmhouse.

"I understand you want to sell your place for $7,500," I began when an elderly gentleman answered the door."

"Nope, I want $7,000," he replied. Maybe he thought that was a higher amount; I'm not sure. But I immediately fetched my checkbook from the car and wrote a check for $200 as a good faith deposit.

I explained that I didn't have a clue about the procedure in buying real estate, but that I loved his old place at first sight, and would be back the next day with a proper agreement. I later learned that a realtor and his customer arrived that same afternoon to make an offer on the farm, but the farmer had told them, "Nope, I made a deal to sell the place this morning."

Over the next couple weeks, I checked the title, obtained a loan for half the price by pledging my few stock shares at the bank, and acquired the farm. I did, meanwhile, ask a good friend if he thought I was doing the right thing, and he replied that he'd give me just twenty-four hours to commit or he'd buy it himself. So I had my assurance.

That transaction was to change the direction of my life in many wonderful ways.

At the closing, the old farmer presented me with some additional costs: the potbelly stove in the parlor would cost me an extra $25; the refrigerator in the kitchen, circa 1937, came to another $25, and the screens were also $25. That seemed to be a standard price for anything that wasn't nailed down and for some things that were. (As for the refrigerator, it's still running.)

At length, he asked if he could keep his hay in the little two-stall barn he had built out back when his main barn had burned down two years previously. I said, sure he could continue to store it and come fetch it in a couple of months when he'd relocated.

A few weeks later he stopped by to ask if that barn was really important to me and could he have it if he could come and move it.

Well, if a 76-year-old man wanted to disassemble and move a small barn he'd built himself, how could I say no? So I agreed: he could come and take the barn when he could arrange for a flat-bed trailer. A couple more weeks down the line he again stopped by to say, "I've decided I don't need the barn after all. Guess I'll sell it to you."

"Well," I protested, "I don't have much money left.

HOW I BOUGHT MY FARM AND HAPPENED INTO A REAL ESTATE CAREER

How much will it cost me?"

He pulled on his chin, said he'd put a lot of work and lumber into that structure, and finally reckoned he'd have to get at least $25. So I gave in and wrote out another of my numerous $25. checks and bought the barn for the second time. But, you see, we both won. He hornswoggled the flatlander and in the process gave me a wonderful anecdote to share.

As I've said, buying that old farmhouse was really a turning point in my life. The house was in dire need of rebuilding and so was I. Ergo the house and I sort of got well together.

The former owners had virtually lived like they'd never emerged from the 19th century. There was one source of cold water pumped into an iron sink from a stoned well under the shed. Under the same shed, 22 feet away, was the outdoor privy, and it was a miracle that the tenants hadn't poisoned their water and themselves.

The electricity was supplied by one line that came in over the front door, took one circuit around the first floor tacked to the ceiling, and back out the front door. Not so surprising, for Gregg Hill hadn't gotten electricity until 1947 with the Rural Electrification Act.

There was no bathtub or shower. The house was not insulated and the only heat sources were the potbelly stove in the living room and the woodburning range. How that farm family survived their 27 severe Vermont winters of ownership is beyond my grasp. And judging from the condition of the buckled foundation and oft-patched roof, I think the house might have been down around their ankles in another year or two.

But it was just the project I needed. I didn't know one end of a hammer from the other. Suburban New York and downtown Manhattan hadn't equipped me for the project, but "necessity being the mother of invention," I quickly learned what was needed.

I was also fortunate to land the help of a wonderful old Vermont carpenter, Norm Houston. Unlike the specialists of today, Norm could do it all. He was:

my plumber	my carpenter
my architect	my roofer
my teacher	my friend

Norm showed me how to jack up the house and replace stones in the classical old foundation. He fed my thin body through a hole in the L-shaped foundation so that I (and the snakes and spiders) could thread electric wire through the crawl space to inaccessible sections of the house. I would tap from below the sub-flooring and Norm would drill from above and fish out the wiring. He also anticipated that we mustn't level the house completely lest it prevent most of the doors from closing, so house jacking was done very sparingly.

When I agonized over the size and shape of dormers for my roof to get much needed light into the upstairs, we concluded that size, shape, and location would be critical for a small house. So Norm made dummy dormers, climbed up on the roof, and moved them to my commands from a vantage point 200 feet away, "till we got it just right."

Norm showed me tricks like using the thick ends of shingles against the wall to help level warped sub-flooring. He also showed me how to strap and insulate the inside walls of my old plank house. Norm even helped lower me down the old 22-foot stoned well to pull up buckets of accumulated sludge and then run gallons of Clorox through the system to help make the water fit to drink.

In essence, Norm saved me from many mistakes that would be the lot of builders not familiar with the idiosyncrasies of old Vermont farmhouses, and he made the experience a joy and a learning process.

Then, came a stunning surprise. When we opened up one of the walls to decide how to go about trying to insulate the place, I made two wonderful discoveries. First, the house was constructed of planks two feet wide and two inches thick that were tenoned and mortised into the slots of the beams above and below, and it was a pre-fab—that is, all the planks had been roman-numeraled, indicating that they had been measured and tenoned in advance of erection, so they would fit into the mortises. You see, the plank house pre-dated the two-by-four studded walls we use today, and therefore left no natural space for insulation.

The second discovery came when I fished out some pieces of newspaper which had been stuffed between the planks and found the recurrent dates to be February and March 1825. My gosh, my house had been built when the United States was only 50 years old, the year when James Monroe relinquished the presidency to John Quincy Adams, and DeWitt Clinton started building the Erie Canal next door in New York State.

One of the bits of newsprint referred to "Clinton's Ditch" or "Clinton's Folly." Now, almost 168 years later, another Clinton has made the political headlines; little could they have guessed.

What wonderful tales that old house could tell, if it could speak. For instance, I learned that at one time in its history, it belonged to Dan Jones, a one-legged Civil War veteran who shared the place with a "scarlet" woman out of wedlock. Dan was apparently quite a rebellious character for this time, and I'm still listening for him to make himself known, like Cora, who's reputed to haunt one of the neighbor houses. The Villa Tragura

Finding the remains of the old barn foundation in a couple of places, I've also become a compulsive stone wall builder. The old house seemed perched precariously atop Gregg Hill once the rotting shed was removed, so I've surrounded it, over the years, with fieldstone walls that impart a sense of solidity bespeaking what Vermont is really made of. It's cost me dearly in pains and strains and trips to Dr. Lincoln Jacobs, the local osteopath, but I can never pass a streambed without looking for the odd flat stone that I can roll up into my car and fetch home to "Hunger Acres."

The renovation of the old place that I've dubbed "Hunger Acres" has been going on by fits and starts for 29 years as time and money have allowed, and may go on for another 29 years, Lord willin'. It's still pretty rude by modern standards, but my wealthier friends don't seem put off and I wouldn't trade it for the Taj Mahal.

Of course, the other fortuitous effect of the place was its leading me into real estate. People seemed to think that my acquisition of that farm was a stroke of genius; so I began pursuing such real estate opportunities for other people. It's fascinating how those serendipitous turns in the road can open whole new spheres. I never did sell anything to my affluent friends back in Larchmont, but I was destined to deal with hundreds of other interesting characters over the years.

Kirby

Chapter 2

In many respects I'm a loner, and I was warned at business school about the pitfalls along the slippery slope of partnership. So my first eight years in real estate were spent as a lone eagle. I had a natural affinity for forests, meadows, and streams, so over the months I walked hundreds of miles of Vermont's countryside studying the qualities of the land, its access, views, and terrain. I became something of an authority on land acquisition, with a minor in residential structures.

Then, Bob Kirby, whom I'd long admired as the owner of the Yodler Lodge, acquired his real estate license. Bob was the type of character with the magnetic personality that everyone wanted to be around. I also knew him to have a natural love and grasp of residential real estate acquired thru his past experience in purchasing and renovating houses.

I couldn't help but think that we'd complement one another as an ideal team, but I hesitated to approach him because I was afraid the admiration might run only one way. However, a mutual friend called suggesting that

Kirby might like to work with me, so I initiated contact, and before we knew it, we had set up office in an old house Kirby owned on the Mountain Road, across from the Yodler known as the Echo. We were both apprehensive about a partnership commitment, so we agreed to join forces on a "two-week cancelable" basis. He technically worked for me, but in reality we were a partnership from the word go. Whoever I didn't know personally in the area, Kirby did, and in no time "the land office was doing a land-office business."

I guess my antipathy to partnership until that time had been the apprehension that I wouldn't be strong enough, vis-à-vis a partner, to stand up for my opinions and my share of the pie. Those fears were quickly and resoundingly dispelled. *If Diogenes was looking for one honest and generous man, it must have been Kirby.* Our only recurrent difference of opinion was that I thought he should take a greater share of our mutual earnings than he did.

Besides that, he proceeded, very subtly, to organize and systemize the office. Before I knew it, we had developed from a couple of free-lance characters to a respected organization. Kirby accomplished it all while he was still technically my employee. Of course, I rectified the situation to an equal partnership as soon as the real estate law would allow; but meanwhile it was a classic case of the tail wagging the dog.

Our eight years of association really enhanced my faith in my fellowman and taught me a profound lesson. If you invest belief in your associates, grant them authority to accompany responsibility, respect their individuality, keep criticism constructive and your mind open to change, then they can become amazingly generous, productive, and nurturing. For me, partnership was a great teacher.

But Kirby was also a uniquely independent and idiosyncratic character. Though quite universally popular, he was, at his core, a very private person. So to moderate the intimacy of our business relationship, he would consistently keep our personal lives at arm's length. For instance, after we had been working together for a year, he threw a large dinner party at the Ten Acres Lodge. In calling the office to accept his invitation, a number of his friends happened to reach me. I took their messages of acceptance. By the end of the week, I came to the stunning realization that I was not going to be invited to the party. My partner, with whom I worked daily, was having a major party for mutual friends, and I wasn't invited. I felt rejected and hurt.

Then an unusual thing happened.

As Kirby owned the building out of which Murray Real Estate operated, he kept an apartment upstairs. One night I was working quite late at my desk when I realized he was up those stairs, with his door open, dreaming and talking in his sleep. It became obvious that he was at a Realtor's meeting in his dream, and he was upset that the membership had failed to take a clear stand on an issue. Suddenly, he very firmly and audibly said, "There's only one person in this organization worth his salt, and you know who that is. It's Bob Murray!"

I remember turning beet red with embarrassment at

having heard his private somnolent utterance. But the next day, I realized how important my inadvertent eavesdropping had been. I realized that, even if I wasn't about to receive the overt affection of my partner, at least I had his respect. That respect and the fun of working with this unique man were enough to sustain our business relationship for the next seven years.

Kirby's reserve of inner privacy manifested itself in other ways. Having been a beloved ski lodge owner over the years, he had a great pool of former lodgers and friends who would arrive in Stowe expecting to stay with him or generally share their visit with him. In defense of his privacy, he actually acquired a house that had only one bedroom, and kept an up-to-date list of recommended alternative lodging and activities for his presumptuous friends.

Kirby had also learned, early on, that the bane of many real estate showings is the two or three kids that Mom or Dad bring along when they are out looking at properties.

In many restaurants, the noise level generated by children, to which the parents have become desensitized, can become very distracting to the couple trying to conduct an intimate tête-à-tête at the next table. Similarly, when a Realtor is trying to impart a large amount of factual data to a prospective buyer and is temporarily dominating the parent's attention, the child in the back seat can become quite insecure, causing an escalating competition between child and broker for Mom's attention. It can be a very trying process when you're reduced to virtually shouting at your prospect. So Kirby made a hard-and-fast rule: children may remain and play with the designated toys in the office or Mom can follow in her own car with the children, but like W.C. Fields, who is purported to have spiked Baby LeRoy's orange juice, he simply refused to enter into competition with the young cherubs.

In our early months, Kirby and I had a couple of disappointing experiences with young women hired as receptionists. In a resort area, their priorities are quite naturally: boyfriends, skiing, and then employment—in that order. After a couple of unsuccessful tries, we had finally opted for a part-time, mature woman and a telephone answering device.

Then late one evening at home, attired in my bathrobe, I answered an unexpected knock on my door, and there stood a vision of young, blond loveliness in a modified miniskirt. Whispering a sub rosa thanks to God, I invited her in only to find she had come seeking a job in real estate. Seems she had recently passed the Vermont broker's exam and had heard that ours was a really convivial office. Trying not to show my disappointment at the purpose of her visit, I explained that my partner had developed an unfortunate aversion to very young women in the office and that I simply couldn't avail myself of her services. I did promise that I would mention the situation to my partner before pronouncing a final no.

Next day I related the visit to Kirby and drew a predictable, "Look, if you want to hire her, train her, be responsible for her, and keep her out of my way, then that's your prerogative." With that great well of warm encouragement, I advised Gretchen that she could come in on weekends and we would try to work her into the system.

What a surprise we were both in for! Turned out this "sweet, naive young waif" had graduated top of her class at Rochester University, possessed somewhat more grey matter than either Kirby or I, and was a self-starter needing very little direction. The upshot was, that within a couple of weeks, she and Kirby had developed a conspiratorial bond that I could hardly penetrate. She was a consummate asset and a joy, and was subsequently to become Vermont Commissioner of Banking and Insurance. I think one of the saddest days in Kirby's life was when she left us to attend law school. You just can't tell a book by its cover, even if the cover stops just above the knees.

Other Kirby stories are legion. One of them reflects the fact that Bob, although one of the kindest, most generous people I knew, had fallen out with his ancestral Catholicism and found a lot of hypocrisy in organized religion. Although I was a flawed, clay-footed Christian, and fully aware of my imperfection, I think there was always a subtle suspicion that I might harbor some holier-than-thouedness under my tolerant exterior.

So when Kirby returned from a trek in the Himalayas one spring, and we had the occasion to be seated at either end of a realtor's conference banquet table at Ten Acres Lodge, fortified with a scotch or two, he made the solemn pronouncement that, having looked into comparative Eastern religions he'd concluded that "Christianity was on the very lowest rung."

At that moment, God must have inspired me with the words, because I spontaneously responded that, "by my yardsticks, Kirby you're the best Christian in Stowe." Without another word, he stiffened, got up from the table, and left the meeting. The interesting thing is that I didn't mean to "hoist him on his own petard." I really believed my assessment of his qualities.

Quite coincidentally, I was to evoke another religious note in our relationship when Kirby was called on the carpet by the Realtor Board's ethics committee for a technical advertising violation. Ironically, the agent who had cited the alleged offense had a reputation for the most questionable ethics on the board, while Kirby was known for his blunt honesty. As the proceedings were petering out for the lack of a clear-cut breach, I found myself quite spontaneously interjecting, "May I suggest 'that he who is without sin cast the first stone' " . . . and on that all-too-appropriate note, the hearing just slowly dissolved.

Kirby possessed one of the greatest senses of humor of our times . . . he would enter a room or a party, and within a very few minutes, an otherwise funereal atmosphere would erupt into spontaneous laughter . . . it was truly a gift. Then one spring I happened to be planning a thirty-day trip to the British Isles, and at a friend's behest I was talked into visiting Mrs. Laferia, a clairvoyant farm lady in Plainfield, Vermont. (Plainfield is well on the other side of the Worcester Mountain Range and quite remote from Stowe.) This lady had become aware, even as a very young girl, that she had a special gift for locating her friends' lost objects, and this ability had developed to a point where she had aided authorities in locating missing persons and had participated in criminal cases. Yet she was a very modest, genteel farm lady who refused to take more than $10.00 per consultation lest she lose her gift.

From the moment I met Mrs. Laferia, I felt an extrasensory communication. She unerringly described my current romantic situation and then reflected that I would forthwith be traveling to England. After we had run over the allotted time by almost an hour and she had refused to take additional money, I was finally saying goodbye at her farm kitchen door. For some reason, I said, "Now that you've correctly surmised that I'm going to England for a sojourn, do you have any feeling about how my partner will fare with our business in the meantime?" Having no way of directly knowing who my partner was or even what our business was, she didn't respond to my question but merely replied, "Doesn't he have the most infectious laughter?" I left that farm in a sense of awe: in one phrase she had described the Kirby that she had never met or heard of.

Kirby and I finally broke up the office and the partnership after eight years. We had actually become too successful for my liking, and I was often working more feverishly than I had in New York. Gretchen decided to pursue the world of law and politics, and Kirby headed west to California, Alaska, and eventually the state of Washington. I returned to a reduced, lone-eagle operation, but the partnership had been a joyful learning experience for me, and we sure-as-hell never had to invoke that two-week cancellation clause. I hope he's having the time of his life in the beautiful Northwest. I miss him!

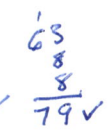

"The Reluctant Panther"

Chapter 3

Back in '69 I was elected president of the Lamoille County Realtor's Association. In those days, the Vermont Realtor's Assoc. was much less active and sophisticated than it is today. Nonetheless, we did get together from time to time to share ideas on how we could best cooperate with one another; keep sight of honesty and the Golden Rule; and try to give something back to our communities. Considering the total amount of commissions up-for-grabs in the Vermont real estate market, I remain amazed at the high degree of fairness and decency that exists between competitive brokers in our area. You can still be generous and ethical and make a successful living.

In May 1970 a statewide meeting was called to be held at the Equinox House in Manchester, Vermont of the realty board heads from all corners of the state. May is the "off" season in Vermont, when the mountain snows and attendant skiing have petered out and the "summer folks" haven't arrived yet. Spring can be a very reluctant bridegroom in Vermont. Even April usually "comes in like a lion . . . and goes out like a lion." Lots of surprise wet snowfalls, and some real nighttime dives by the thermometer. But by the middle of May, spring has finally sprung with all the vernal burgeoning of woods and fields, and the sunny days that promise renewal of nature and pe haps even romance. Thus I was full of anticipation of an idyllic, three-day sojourn to the little Village of Manchester, nestled in the shadow of Mt. Equinox. For a few days I'd be free of any pressing responsibilities, and able to savor that wonderful sense of comparative anonymity.

Then "Old Scratch" laid his hex on me. The vice president of the Lamoille County Realtors that year happened to be a fine, hard-working, ethical fellow . . . but he also happened to be the ultimate back-slapping, hale-fellow-well-met kind of guy that one pictures giving out exploding cigars at a Shriner's convention. He jolted me out of my reverie, by announcing that he'd decided to join me at the convention. I sensed immediately that my idyllic bubble had burst. Fortunately, I did have the presence of mind to invent a side business sortie en route that precluded the "enjoyment" of his driving company to and from Manchester. But on the Friday evening of my arrival at the Equinox House, sure enough, Jim was there to shout his greeting across the full width of the hotel lobby and to advise that he'd saved me an honored place at his table for dinner. A cloud of gloom settled over my shoulders, and I wished for some quieter place like Times Square. When the interminable dinner was over and I had endured Jim's questionable jokes and repetitive anecdotes, his sense of camaraderie had just been whetted.

"What-da-ya-say we head downtown and see if there's any action in this social outpost," was his suggestion.

I thanked him for his offer, but as diplomatically as possible, explained that my plans were to get the Burlington Free Press, catch up on the news, and turn in very early.

"You take care of the carousing for both of us; I don't want to be late for that important 9 a.m. session tomorrow." He accepted my reply and we both headed our separate ways.

But when I stopped at the front desk, the clerk advised that they'd run out of newspapers and that I'd have to stop at the stationery store in the village. No problem, I like to walk or jog after dinner, so I headed off to the village for my constitutional and my paper. On my way back, with my newspaper tucked dutifully under my arm, my attention was captured by a most unique sign . . . "The Reluctant Panther Inn and Restaurant." What especially stopped me was the painting on the signboard of a most seductive creature; half woman - half panther. I've always been curious about the feline qualities of some women, so I was almost subconsciously lured to peek into the place.

When I walked into the establishment, I was immediately struck by the mural-size painting of a Naked Lady & Two Panthers above the bar. The artist had certainly concocted a most alluring, visceral, nubile creature. The quickening of my pulse was compounded by a sultry voice from behind the bar asking me what I would have to drink.

Now, perhaps my imagination played tricks on me, but I swear I was looking at the personification of the Reluctant Panther. I started to explain that I was on my way to early bed, but when the words emerged they sounded more like, "I'll have Dewars on the rocks." Well, I rationalized, one little drink wouldn't hurt and I wouldn't be lying to my friend because I sat down at the bar and opened the Burlington Free Press to the real estate section.

Then, as if this had all been plotted by Beelzebub himself, my eyes focused on an object behind the bar . . . a guitar . . . a Martin D-28 at that.

"Do you play the guitar as well as tend bar?" I asked the panther.

"Oh, my no," she replied, "a friend of the owner left it here when he went to Florida. Do you play?"

"Well, actually my guitar has paid the rent in some of my leaner years," I admitted, and before I knew it, she had taken it down and handed it to me.

Well, a guitar can be an amazing catalyst, and to make a long story short, it turned out to be one of those rare spontaneous nights. I sang all the Vermont ditties I had written over the years, did the Tom Lehrer, Simon & Garfunkel, and Peter, Paul & Mary stuff, and finally the few romantic ballads in my repertoire. By one a.m. like Bobby McGee, I'd "sung up all the songs that lady knew," brought the curious in from the restaurant section, greatly augmented the tips of "the Pantheress," and prevailed upon her to join me for a nightcap.

By 1:15 a.m., after putting the bar to bed, an absolutely smashing creature slid into my car and melted me with a feline sinuous move to my side.

As this was her home bailiwick, we decided it would be advisable to drive up to a little mountain inn in an adjoining town where she'd be less likely to encounter her compatriots. Hell, at that stage I'd have chartered a jet to Paris if that's what she wanted. At any rate, we got to the Peru Inn, ordered a drink, and were deep in intimate conversation across a lamp-lit booth in the corner when I felt a tap on my shoulder.

"So this is your idea of reading the paper and turning in early, eh!"

I was stunned . . . there stood my "hale-fellow-well-met" friend, Jim. I started to explain about having run into an "old family friend," but finally just quoted Robie Burns and sputtered, "the best-laid plans o' mice and men gang aft agley," bought him a drink, and left as quickly as possible for more intimate surroundings.

The next morning I arrived late for that "very important 9 a.m. meeting," and managed to avoid Jim's pointed stare. I tried valiantly to assume a sober attitude, but the implacable smile kept creeping across my face. In truth, I never did get to read the Burlington Free Press . . . and, I shall never again see a panther in a zoo or a circus without experiencing a strong sense of arousal.

Courtesy of Stowe Reporter

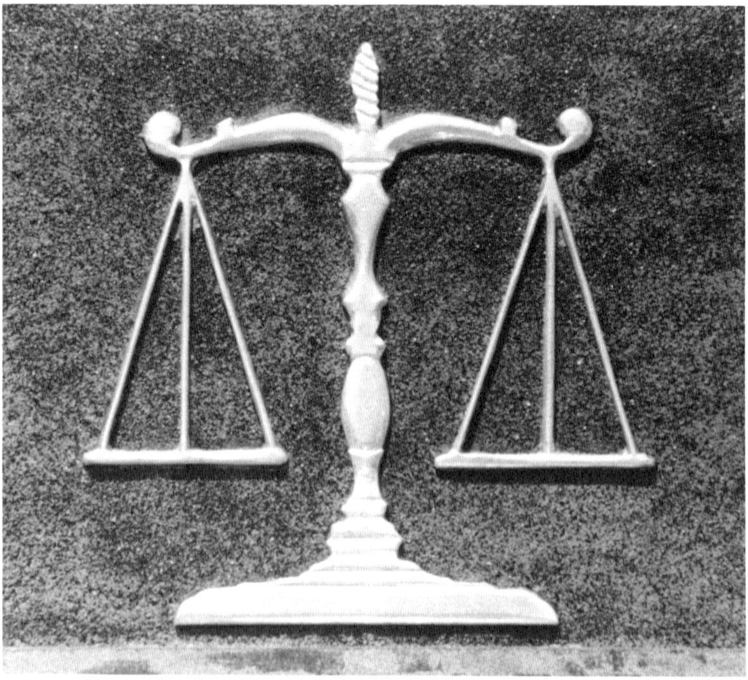

The Post Graduate Paper Chase

Chapter 4

Until I entered real estate, I think I had been in an attorney's office once in my first 30 years. Since then, I've spent about one- third of my business life in their company. I have very ambivalent feelings toward the legal profession. On one hand, they are some of the most capable, hard- working people I know, protecting us from the selfish machinations of our covetous human minds. A good lawyer, through his anticipation, can save us untold grief down the line. Kipling talked of "lesser breeds without the law."

On the other hand, through their preponderance in our legislatures and their proclivity for detail, they espouse the endless laws, regulations, and contractual complications that perpetuate the demand for their services. I've often thought that state and federal legislation should be limited to displacement law—i.e., you can only pass a law if it replaces one of the old laws already clotting up our lives.

Malpractice liability, and harassment litigation are examples of the costly and initiative-numbing proliferation of the law. Law firms are increasingly advertising for clients with real or imagined injury claims. The whole concept of punitive versus compensatory damages has escalated the degree of exposure and the cost of malpractice insurance in many fields to the level that has forced some physicians, for example, to quit delivering babies. We have become, by far, the most litigious society in the world. The new no-fault attitude in life seems to be "heads I win, tails I sue."

The average person or average jury seems to think that the multi-million dollar judgments against business and industry are just paid for by the fat cats or the big corporations that can well afford them. They don't seem to grasp that, in the final analysis, the recent $105,000,000 judgment against General Motors will be paid by everyone who buys a car or pays for insurance for the next twenty years.

There's no question that we need good attorneys to protect the public from the unscrupulous and criminally incompetent operators who bring injury and loss to the innocents with whom they deal. But "caveat emptor" has become a thing of the past, and coverage for every conceivable injustice from an unsuspected, faulty, sub-surface septic system, to *perceived* sexual harassment has become part of the cost of doing business that is ultimately borne by the consumer of the goods or services. I can only hope that eventually jury awards will reflect a sense of proportion to the actual malfeasance or injury sustained.

To be fair, however, human nature being what it is, and real estate often representing the exchange of one man's birthright for another man's life savings, a lot of conflict can develop and a thorough lawyer can anticipate most of these conflicts and liabilities. This led my friend to claim that "a good lawyer is expensive, a poor lawyer is very expensive, and no lawyer can turn out to be prohibitively expensive . . ." whence I needle my attorney friends that they are, unfortunately, a necessary evil.

George King

Of course, real estate law in Vermont was a "fur piece" more informal 25 years ago than it is today. One of my favorite legal practitioners in those days was Attorney George King of Morrisville, Vermont. George held sway in a second floor walk-up office above the barber shop in "downtown" Morrisville. The old wooden stairs leading to this office were worn and dished by many decades of traffic. George, a rather portly man, sat behind his large desk piled high with papers and files. He had a wonderful accessibility; if he was present, he would see you. I tried not to abuse that privilege, by being prepared with the pre-reviewed documents that I wanted to discuss.

His office was a large, barren room with a couple of straight-backed chairs for visitors, probably calculated to preclude the comfort that might tempt one to extend his visit. But the most striking thing about George's office was that, in season, there were stacked many cans of Vermont maple syrup to the right of his desk and bundles of Christmas trees to the left of his desk. In all fairness, this retailing operation helped support and motivate a young son he and his wife, Ruth, had adopted, but although I was never pressured, I did find it hard to leave our conferences without buying at least a pint of maple syrup.

Now, as I've found myself over the ensuing years involved in some fairly sizable transactions that have taken me as far afield as the board rooms of Wall Street, I've been struck by the extravagance of many conference rooms. They often appear to be ego-trips for executives whose realms or scopes hardly justify the grandiloquence of the furnishings. Not so George King: his conference room was only accessible in the summer months or to those sufficiently clothed. George's conference room was an old porch cantilevered off the back of the building which did not have the benefit of a heating system. There's no way I can confirm this, but in my heart I always felt that the "conference room" was George's tongue-in-cheek way of making fun of the pretensions of the sophisticated visitors who from time-to- time found themselves doing business in his modest lair.

George had a couple of other idiosyncrasies that I loved. First, he was cagey enough never to slander either a client or an adversary. In law, as well as real estate, you never know when, down-the-road, you are going to be in the role of an ally of a former adversary. George still had a way of getting his point across if he wanted you to be forewarned about entanglement with an unsavory character. When asked about such a person, George would invariably begin his reply by, "Now, that John

THE POST GRADUATE PAPER CHASE

Jones is a fine fellow . . . I wouldn't necessarily say that honesty is his long suit . . . but on the other hand, if you had your cash in advance," etc. George could succinctly expose a phony without ever using a word of condemnation.

Another of George's unique practices was to hold his real estate closings on the office floor. When an involved closing was to take place, George would requisition some extra chairs from neighboring offices and sit us all in a circle next to his desk. Then on the floor he would place the survey and mapping references in one pile, the title search and lien clearances in another, the proposed deed and transfer papers in a third, etc. Actually, it was a very effective procedure, because all of the elements of the closing were in plain view of all the attendant parties, and as any questions or conflicts arose we could deal with the particular pile germane to the subject.

This floor-closing practice did almost blow a deal of mine in one particular case. The seller of a certain large parcel of land had actually represented his land as 145 acres more-or-less. Back when Vermont land was relatively inexpensive, it was quite common for the owner to take the position "that's about what I got . . . that's what I'm selling . . . you go walk it and decide if you want to buy it . . . but I ain't surveying it and I ain't signing any paper guaranteeing any fixed number of acres." In this case, the buyer had agreed to buy the parcel "as is." But reviewing U.S. Agriculture Department aerial photos with a grid, etc., I had become convinced this was one of those rare instances when there was more, rather than less, acreage in the parcel. The purchaser whom, by

44

buyer/broker contract, I represented in this case, decided to have a survey prior to closing to satisfy his curiosity. Remarkably the land came out to be within one acre of my estimate of 165 acres.

Now, my buyer, having made his deal at the seller's asking price and based on the seller's estimate of acreage, took the position that the survey he paid for was his possession and thus it wasn't to be introduced into the closing, lest it raise issue of increased consideration.

I explained all this to George who represented my buyer, and he agreed that the sale should proceed on the terms of the sales agreement. But in this rare instance, George forgot and dropped the survey plainly indicating 164 acres on the floor, in the midst of our circle of participants. Fortunately, my wits didn't fail me, and I quickly drew attention to the stack of maple syrup and the Christmas trees. By the time the group had again focused on the papers, I had deftly palmed the survey. George quickly picked up on its disappearance and things proceeded to a satisfactory conclusion.

I miss George. He was a colorful character. I'm sure he enjoyed his role as a legal country bumpkin, and mostly I think he delighted in surprising the sophisticates with his deep practical grasp of "the Law." If Solomon is still confronting insoluble legal questions in Heaven and if Attorney Welsh is still dealing with the Senator McCarthys of the afterlife, I'll bet George is at their side giving advice.

A Country Lawyer Saves the Day

Back in 1972, I listed a large farm in Worcester for sale. Much of the land was "ledgy," wet, and poor for farming, but its location, just seven miles north of the state capital of Montpelier bisected by a major state highway, made it a very attractive medium-range investment. I finally convinced a customer from "down country" of the future possibilities, and after extensive negotiations, we finally came to an equitable agreement for the purchase of the farm. This included perpetuation of the farming operation and free tenancy by the farmers for an extended period after purchase.

The owners happened to be two brothers of French Canadian ancestry, and by Vermont community property law, their respective wives. One of the wives was a recent acquisition, having immigrated from nearby Canada, and married brother number two during the previous year. She spoke no English, but had signed the sales agreement on the farm after an explanation by her husband.

The day of the closing we all met in Montpelier at the attorney's office. The conference room was quite crowded, replete with two attorneys, two realtors, two buyers, the two Chouinard brothers . . . and one of the wives. Nervously, I inquired as to the whereabouts of the other Mrs. Chouinard. Quite matter-of-actly, brother number two explained that his wife had decided against signing the deed. I really don't think he realized that without both wives' signatures, the whole deal was null and void.

After much discussion, and with much sadness, eight of the nine people in the room picked up their papers and headed for the exit.

At that point, the shrewd old Yankee lawyer for the sellers said, "Hold on! I suggest before we throw in the towel, we send out for sandwiches from the deli downstairs and have Mr. Murray, enterprising young broker that he is, accompany my secretary, who speaks not only French, but French Canadian patois, on a visit to the second Mrs. Chouinard." He then took me aside and instructed, "Now, this lady is in a new country with an unfamiliar language; she's probably feeling insecure about all this, and she's probably angry that she wasn't sufficiently consulted. You go up there and hear her out. Let her thoroughly vent her spleen, and whatever you do, don't try to talk her into anything."

So while the craggy lawyer regaled the assembled lunchers with sandwiches and tales of his hunting prowess, I headed north, with the French-speaking secretary and with much trepidation, to confront Mrs. Chouinard. Fortunately, I understood enough French to follow the gist of the lively ensuing discussion. The horse sense of the lawyer turned out to be incredibly accurate. We were met with a French barrage of hurt feelings, xenophobia, and irritation. The lawyer's secretary was wonderful; she listened, she sympathized, she empathized, she agreed . . . but not one word was spoken to try and dissuade the lady from her dug-in position.

Then, just as I was despairing of ever seeing a resolution of this road block, Mrs. Chouinard said, "Donnez-moi le papier!" which she promptly signed. She had had her "day in court"; she had asserted herself, she had talked with someone in her own language. Thence, a sense of resignation and calm had come over her.

Bidding our fond adieus, we hurried back to Montpelier (where the "country lawyer" was still spinning his yarns), completed the closing, and headed our separate ways.

As a salesman, I learned a valuable lesson that day. Sometimes your most effective sales strategy is merely to shut up and listen. I've never forgotten that I owe that Yankee lawyer for both a commission and a valuable lesson in human psychology.

The Prince and the Pauper

To Live by the Side of the Road and be a Friend to Man

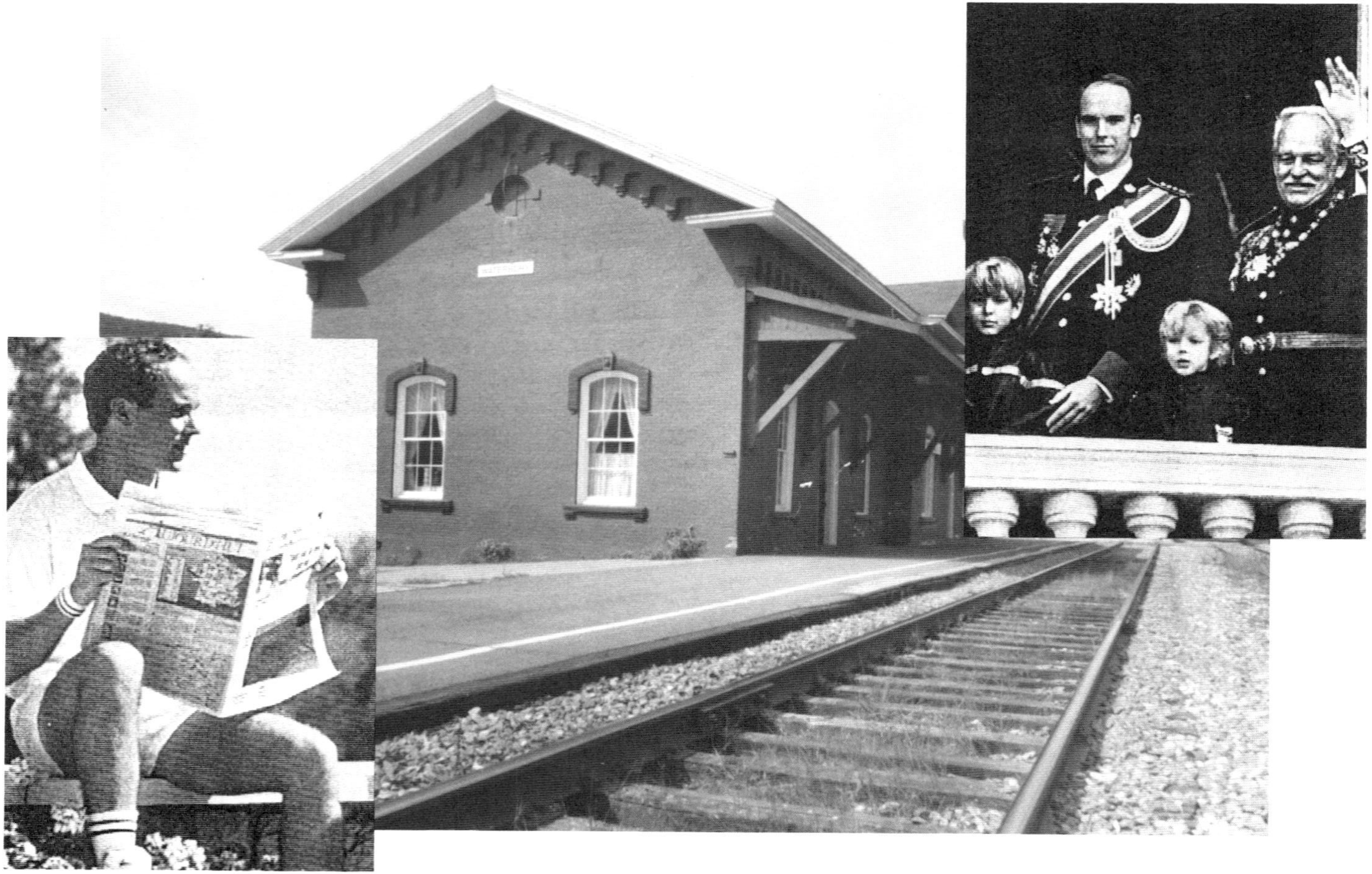

CHAPTER 5

After acquiring and painstakingly renovating my little farmhouse poised atop Gregg Hill, I learned that with the lovely mountain views came the unwritten obligation to come to the aid of my fellowman. Winter storms and spring mud seasons rendered the town road up Gregg Hill a sheet of ice or a quagmire from time to time. Three or four nights each year comes a knock on my door seeking a shovel or a push or a phone. Sometimes some ashes from my wood stove and a shovel will do the trick; sometimes it's coffee or hot chocolate until the wrecker arrives.

One night my charitable instincts moved me to both call for, and pay for, a wrecker for a young man who had just ditched his new pick-up truck. Two days hence, I was informed by the State Police that I had aided and abetted the theft of said vehicle. My good intentions had been sorely misdirected.

Then one morning, on my pre-breakfast jog, I was passing the house at the bottom of the hill (which had been rented out for the winter season to some young

THE PRINCE AND THE PAUPER

skiers), when I took note of a young man replete with overcoat and collegiate scarf, who seemed quite upset. I slowed my pace and called in inquiry of his problem. He explained that the Amtrak train was due at the Waterbury Station in 15 minutes and his promised taxi had not yet arrived. "If you want to run back up to the top of the hill with me, we can jump in my car and make it to your train," I offered. He immediately fell in stride and in no time we were en route. When we made our timely arrival at the station he was most effusive in his thanks, as he had important classes at Amherst College that afternoon. He introduced himself as Albert Grimaldi and said he hoped our paths would cross again.

Driving back home from the station, the name Grimaldi kept ruminating in my mind (in this dairy state, we often ruminate). Then I pulled over and stopped the car. "Holy mackerel! That was Prince Albert of Monaco . . . Grace Kelly's son! . . . that is the family name, right? . . . and the prince is Albert, right?" But had I heard right or was this a case of a little self delusion?

At any rate, I told a few friends about the episode and elicited comments ranging from, "Well, the Prince is known to like winter sports" . . . to the more skeptical, "He probably said Alvin Giraldi or something like that." So questioning myself and realizing that my story was meeting with less and less credibility, I decided to stop mentioning the occurrence.

Then this winter, about eight years after the incident, I got a call from George Lengvari, a good friend and real estate investor from Montreal, to whom I had told the tale back in '86. George had attended the Montreal hockey game the previous evening as part of the Canadian Prime Minister's entourage. Among the group had been a young man from Europe, one Albert Grimaldi, with his French Canadian girl friend. George had had the temerity to approach the Prince about a possible mutual friend in little Waterbury Center, Vermont.

As George related the incident over the phone, I winced and expected that the Prince would have replied, "I've never been in Waterbury, Vermont in my life." But instead he had said, "Why yes, that's the great guy who drove me to the train. He really got me out of a jam; please give him my warmest regards."

George must have been almost as flabbergasted as I was. Of course the real estate implication is that I could now probably sell George the Brooklyn Bridge or the great miasmic swamp. He now believes almost anything I tell him.

But the real moral of this story is more applicable to young ladies. "If you see a frog in trouble by the side of the road, stop and pick him up; he may very well turn out to be a prince."

Courtesy of Stowe Reporter

Being in the Right Place at the Right Time

or

Sometimes It's Not What You Know, but Who You Know

Chapter 6

A few years ago, an old friend in Montreal with the unlikely name of Boris Berbrier phoned me. Boris, bless him, had given my name to one of the most affluent men in Canada who had expressed interest in buying property in the Stowe area.

So, on an appointed morning, I drove up to the Scandinavian Inn to meet this visiting mogul for the purpose of showing him local real estate. En route, it suddenly occurred to me that if this gentleman wasn't familiar with Stowe, I might have a tough time convincing him that I was a significant factor on the Stowe real estate scene. You see, I ran the lowest-profile realty operation in Vermont. I did almost no advertising at the time and had no window-on-Main-Street. How could I, in our short allotted time, impress this guy that I was deep in the fabric of the market without sounding egocentricly immodest.

After picking him up and starting down the Mountain Road, I was ineptly sputtering about my past achievements and present status . . . all of which seemed to be going over like a large cement cloud with my customer, when we were suddenly flagged down on the highway.

"Balls," I thought, "now we're going to be held up by some farmer's cows while I stew in my own juice."

Turned out, it just happened to be the "Stowe Hunt" with its riders and horses and hounds, which, while more colorful than a herd of cows, was equally impeding.

Then fortune smiled on me. As the first rider passed my car, he leaned down from his handsome steed and said . . . "Bob, how the heck are you." The next rider repeated the process to remind me that I was due for cocktails and dinner Friday night. By the time the Stowe Hunt had passed by in its entirety, and I had been greeted by most of the riders, my companion had to know that I was well connected to the market, enabling me to assume my false modesty pose. The need for preferred position in "The Stowe Reporter" and an impressive office had been eliminated. Surreptitiously, I raised my left pinky, looked skyward, and mumbled under my breath . . . "Thank you, Lord."

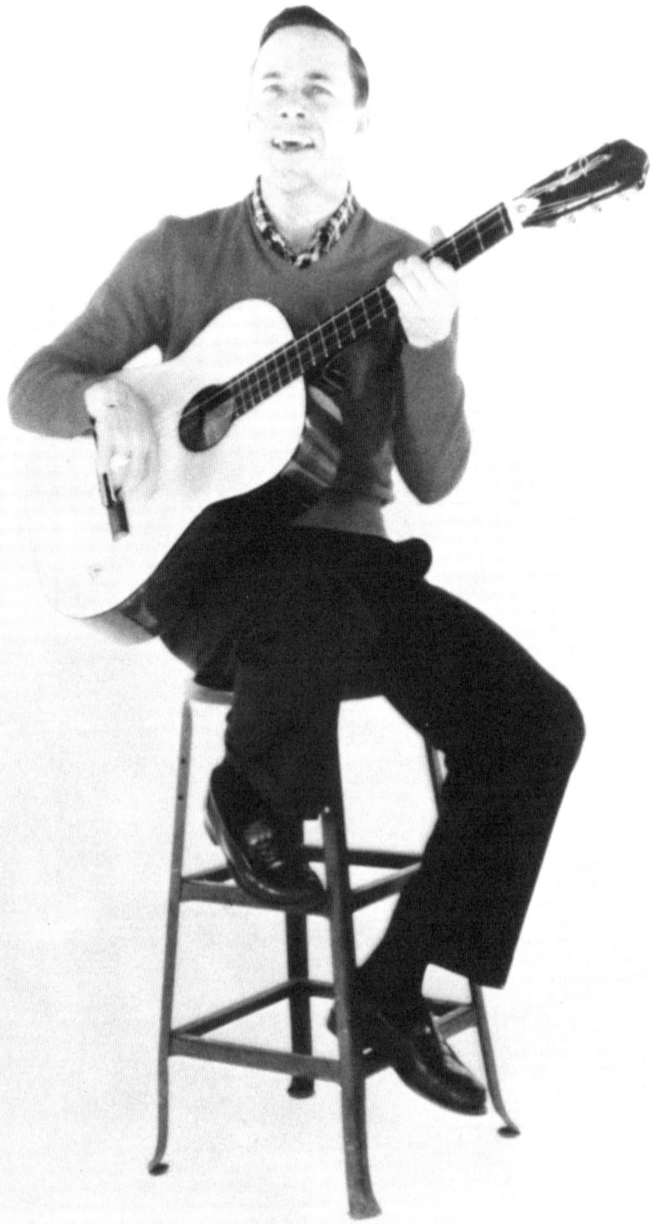

*"The Lord Giveth
and the Lord Taketh Away"*

Chapter 7

When I had been in Vermont a couple of years, had reached the ripe old age of 32, and had just started to try to make a living in real estate, I developed a virtual adolescent crush on the beautiful 22-year-old daughter of the people who owned the Logwood Inn.

My awkward efforts at courting this young damsel were pretty much unrequited and further impeded by her parents who weren't crazy about the attentions of this "older man." Finally, one black day, she informed me that we couldn't see each other anymore, and that there was another man in her life.

I was devastated: my heart ached, my teeth ached, my fingernails ached, and my ego was thoroughly trampled. Of course, we've all suffered that bereft sense of rejection at some time in our lives, but the commonality didn't ease my pain.

On the rebound, I thought of a young lady of comparative vintage to whom I was giving guitar lessons at the time. I figured I'd take her to the country club party that

Saturday night, and perhaps show Miss Logwood that our age difference was not such an impediment.

But arriving at the party with my date, I soon saw the object of my obsession on the arm of a handsome young ski instructor, which caused my pain to intensify, and I quickly suggested to my date that we move on to a party being given by the neighbors of my little renovated farmhouse on Gregg Hill.

These neighbors were two charming, multi-lingual, Canadian brothers recently graduated from McGill University. When we arrived at the Gregg Hill party, we found that they'd assembled an attractive, cosmopolitan group of young people as Montreal is wont to produce. I had, meanwhile, stopped along the way to pick up my guitar and a bottle of champagne.

Upon arrival at the party, I introduced my young friend to the group, but almost before I knew what had happened, I was enlisted to play accompanying guitar chords to all their collegiate songs. It was a lively and extended sing-along, and I thus paid scant attention to the young lady who had accompanied me.

When I finally became aware of my rudeness, I sought her out and was stunned to see that she was deeply engrossed in the repartee of my neighbor and host. They were so engrossed in one another that I think I could have passed a flaming hoop between them without their noticing. Now my ego was really flattened; I had apparently lost two women in the same weekend.

But I had few moments to contemplate my state of abject rejection, because at that juncture an attractive young lady from England asked if I'd like to dance. Heck, at that point I'd have jumped at the chance to dance with my old maid aunt. However, we'd barely made one turn around the floor when she whispered, "I have a terrible crush on you." Blushing I took evasive action and countered that with a couple more inches of snow "the skiing should be quite good in the morning."

"You're not listening," she insisted, "I have a real thing for guitar players, and you really rattle my cage."

Flabbergasted, I said to myself, "How could she be taken with a 32-year old has been, who's just been rejected by two women?"

Then before I could sputter any further, someone ran through the front door to report that Charlie Hart, the special honored and expected guest of the evening, had just ditched his car on the way up the icy Gregg Hill Road . . . all able-bodied people were conscripted to pull Charlie out of the ditch. Sensing that I had been delivered from a very embarrassing situation, I grabbed my parka and the English girl, and headed out the front door. But once outside, there was a firm tug on my sleeve away from Charlie's predicament to create one of my own. We headed for the adjacent guest chalet.

I later learned that she was on the rebound, estranged from a husband back in Montreal. Buttressed by spirits fermenti, she had decided I was at least a temporary answer to her problems. So we proceeded to bring great solace, reassurance, and pleasure to one another in that empty chalet. It was a delightful and thoroughly gratifying interlude, but when we awoke from our tryst, lying on the chalet's newly carpeted floor, the dawn was breaking over the mountain, and reality was breaking in my mind.

Oh, my God, what have I done? I had abandoned the lovely young thing I'd brought to the party . . . I had insulted my host by making off with one of his friends wives . . . and to compound the felony, my companion was completely unrepentant and insisted on singing all the way back to the main house, twirling her panties, and extolling my prowess as a lover.

At 6:30 a.m. having kissed her good morning, and deposited her in the main house, I tiptoed out and headed for my own abode across the road. I found myself exhausted, but I was hardly in the mood for sleep. I was terribly confused about whether I possessed great sex appeal or none at all . . . I was very concerned about the major social gaffe of failing to escort my date home . . . and I had no idea what kind of involvement I had precipitated with a female I hardly knew.

I had just begun to consider whether I would have to leave Gregg Hill if not the State. Lord Chesterfield's admonition kept running thru my brain . . . "The cost is exorbitant, the position ridiculous and the pleasure transitory."

Then the phone rang . . . it was my neighbor's voice on the other end . . . now I was going to have to face the music . . . now comes divine retribution!

"Bob, Phil here," he opened. "I can't tell you how sorry I am old chap; I had the extremely bad taste to make off with your date last night. Can you forgive me?"

Could I forgive him? You better believe I could! What a sense of relief. Apparently, my partner of the previous evening had weighed more soberly the possible consequences of our indiscretion, and our night of lovemaking hadn't been revealed to the other guests. Phil's only concern was with his own bad form. Fate had given me at least a partial reprieve.

I did call my original date of the evening to apologize for my failure to escort her home, but sensed very little reaction or wounded pride from the other end of the phone conversation.

The reason for her nonchalance became apparent in the ensuing weeks. For her and Phil, it had been the proverbial thunderbolt . . . a true case of love at first sight. Within six months of the fateful party, they were man and wife.

There was a double irony. My neighbor, Phil, had led me to acquire my beloved farm on Gregg Hill, and now I had led him to the girl who was to become his wife . . . the ledger was balanced.

From the Pages of Horatio Alger

Paul
Reed ?

CHAPTER 8

Money is hardly the only reward of the real estate business. Being a catalyst to someone's achievement and sharing the unfolding of a success story can be just as rewarding. And often it's that synergy of a person with entrepreneurial spirit and the facilitating efforts of a caring broker that makes it all happen, whence money, if it comes, is merely a by-product.

John came to me a few years back when he was just 21 years old. He was a 1st year college dropout from Berkeley who was impatient to leave the academic womb to try his hand at the free enterprise system. When I met him, he was marking time while eking out a living as a ward attendant at the State Hospital in Waterbury.

John was a handsome, disarming, albeit impecunious young man. He said he could round up about $8,000 and wanted to buy a building site in Stowe. Land was less expensive back then, but even so there was only one pre-approved parcel of land in all of Stowe at that price. It was just 0.99 acres, heavily wooded, with no proven

Confessions of a Vermont Realtor

From the Pages of Horatio Alger

view nor source of water . . . but hope springs eternal in the youthful breast, so John put down his meager savings and proceeded to try to build his first house. He began by clearing the building site and saving the best logs for the mill, so the house could be built of its own indigenous timber.

After we'd finalized the land purchase, and because, fortunately, this was not my largest real estate transaction of the year, I got involved in several other directions. Then I happened to run into John some months later skiing at the mountain.

"Hi, Bob, I've built the house and now I'm ready to have you sell it for me."

"Oh, my God," I thought, "this kid has probably built something resembling a treehouse, and now I'm saddled with the painful chore of bursting his balloon and explaining that his amateurish efforts are not salable in this sophisticated resort market." However, I dutifully and reluctantly trudged over to view the carnage.

As I pulled up to the site, I could see that the modified salt box was no beautiful swan, but on the other hand, it did look like it was likely to remain standing for some time, and . . . the clearing work had opened a surprising view of the mountains.

As I entered the little vestibule, I was pleased to find that the door closed snugly. Next I was struck by a gleaming, matched- maple hardwood floor, and as each part of the house unfolded, I was pleasantly surprised to find that my young friend had built a very efficient, though modest, three-bedroom, two-bath house, with poured concrete basement, gas heat, built-in kitchen cabinetry, etc.

I felt equal amounts of pleasure and relief at being able to promise John that we could market the house at a reasonable profit. Of course, he had every cent he could beg, borrow or steal in the project, so I had to loan him the $230.00 to get his car out of hock, but eventually we did get the place sold; I got my $230 back and a modest commission; and John had proven both to me and to himself that he could undertake such a project from scratch and make it happen.

John then headed west to Alta, Utah for some high altitude skiing and much deserved R & R, and I returned to my more conventional clientele. Then about six months later on a Sunday afternoon in May, I was mowing my lawn when a pick-up truck pulled into the drive . . . 'twas John back from the Rockies. Being a man of great frugality where words are concerned, he said, "Hi, I'm back . . . got any building jobs?"

As most of the major construction contracts for that summer were monopolized by the established building firms in town, I was not able to be encouraging to my young friend. Then an idea dawned.

I had received a call from a New Jersey divorce attorney, advising me that a youngish divorcee with five kids had just received a handsome divorce settlement and had the crazy idea that she could build a log cabin in Vermont and involve all the kids from twelve to twenty-one. She figured she could achieve the idyllic vacation home in beautiful Vermont and bind the family together all in one fell swoop.

"John, how would you like a job as half builder, half camp counsellor?" I asked.

"Sure, I'll give anything a try," he said, and so we were off to the races.

Now the lady turned out to be a former Miss New Hampshire, and one of the most striking 40ish women that it's been my pleasure to behold. The kids, including a ranking national junior tennis player, were equally attractive and enthusiastic, so I ferreted out a beautiful 10-acre lot on the Elmore Mt. Road at the ultimate bargain price of $19,000. It had a pristine mountain stream running diagonally through the property, so we found a site strategically overlooking the stream, and all of us proceeded to clear the lot, tote stones for the wall, search for a spring, design and cut the driveway, site the septic area, etc. It was sort of a Swiss Family Robinson operation and the family actually lived in a tent on the property in the early phases of the operation. Their only fear was that a bear might knock on their tent flaps some frosty morning, and I was sorely tempted to fake the intrusion. I did buy a life-size stuffed bear, but in the end rejected the idea for fear of causing apoplexy.

Later on, efforts in "the field" were rewarded by wine and spaghetti dinners at a rented apartment in Stowe pending completion of the house. The family involvement was great fun (a veritable reprise on my youth) and it was so basically satisfying to be involved in every phase of the operation, from finding the land to seeing the house take shape and become occupied. I really believe every realtor should get involved in the "hands-on" building of a structure at some time in his career. After all, the home or structure is the end result of our marketing efforts and I think it's vitally important to experience their ultimate fruition.

Of course, as in any idyllic concept, many problems arose in the unfolding of the building project. Trying to involve five youngsters without professional building skills, and arbitrate over internecine spats, caused great frustration for poor John. Nonetheless, the log house eventually got built, commanding a lovely view of the stream and pond.

John and the owner parted a little sadder but wiser for the growing pains of such a family project. As for me, I learned a great deal about the joys and problems of the building process, and still cherish wonderful memories of spaghetti dinners with a great bunch of kids. Oh, incidentally, my total income for the year's involvement was $950, my co-broker fee on the sale of the land. I figure that came to about $2.70 per hour over the life of the project . . . but I wouldn't have traded the experience for the world.

After that fascinating episode, I once again, lost track of John for a few months. Rumor had it, he had bought a large tract of land but I wasn't involved. Then driving along the Randolph Road in Morristown one day, I caught sight of John's ancient Volvo up on the side of a hill at a clearing leading to a high wooded area. Anxious to see my friend, I drove up the hill and found him stripped to the waist, felling some major trees. Turned out he had acquired 211 acres for the grand total of $50,000 with only 25% down in cash. He had then bought a second-hand bulldozer and proceeded to build 3/4's of a mile of private road into this beautiful tract of woods and meadow. John's initiative just never ceased to amaze me.

However, he had hit that juncture that causes many young investors to come-a-cropper. He had a great parcel of land, a find road . . . and no money with which to complete the project. Besides, state and town environmental laws were about to kick-in and cause months of costly delays in applications, legal fees, etc. So John laid the problem at the feet of his trusty realtor. "You know, for the right price I'd sell this place," said John. It may have been a masterpiece of understatement by my cool young friend. With the costs and delays facing him, he could have lost the whole ball of wax.

Well, the gods were smiling on us again. Almost simultaneously Ray Cabral, owner of a large management consulting firm, came to me looking for peripheral tracts of land in the general vicinity of Stowe. Ray could see that Stowe was growing and he had the wherewithal to invest on the fringes and await Stowe's inevitable expansion. John didn't have the luxury of waiting, but he could turn his initiative, his fortunate installment purchase, and his hard work into a very handsome short-term profit. He also had the smarts to do one other strategic thing; he had built himself a modest log house on the land, and while working on the road, had actually lived there for the preceding year. It meant he could sell the property at a substantial profit and defer his exposure to the IRS capital gains tax by re-investing in a primary residence within two years of the sale.

We finally worked out a veritable Ponzi transaction. We put a value of $225,000.00 on John's land, and Ray swapped him his lovely new spec house on Birch Hill in Stowe at a value of $195,000 plus $30,000 in cash. John, temporarily, had a luxurious place to live (sans furniture) and 30 G's in his pocket; Ray had a great future investment. We then successfully sold the Birch Hill house, and, although reduced to very modest living conditions once again, John suddenly was a 25 year old with an approximate net worth of $170,000.

Not content to rest on his oars, with the kind of net worth it takes many a lifetime to accumulate, John continued to expand his activities, establishing the Little River Mill Works with a fellow builder who happens to be a genius in woodworking machinery; acquiring a 160 acre parcel of magnificent land on the Elmore Mt. Road with two co-investors that I produced from Paris and Montreal; and purchasing a prime building site in Stowe Hollow. He had followed the advice that Texas billionaire Clint Mercheson had given to his sons . . . "money's like manure; it doesn't do any good unless you spread it around."

Well, John had spread it around, all right, but once again he needed an infusion of working capital. So off we went to the bank to apply for a building loan for a house on his newly-acquired building lot in the hollow.

The banker was very cordial, but her first question was "What is your monthly income . . . and what has been your average salary over the last three years?"

John's frank reply was, "I don't have a monthly income, and I've never really had a salary. I've netted about $170,000 over the last two years, but that doesn't seem to fit any of the blanks on your questionnaire."

Try as she could, the banker didn't seem to be able to fit John into her application formula. Her bosses, and particularly the secondary mortgage market into which John's mortgage would be sold, had to attest to a predictable earning pattern from which John could be expected to pay off his note.

So, sadly, we walked out of the bank empty handed. I turned to John and said, "You've probably made three times as much as that banker for the last two years, but unfortunately, you are not a mortgageable commodity."

It was beginning to look like my young friend had accomplished a "meteoric rise to mediocrity" when I was reminded of an old acquaintance, who, by dint of hard work and steely nerves, had become president of a growing bank in a neighboring town. I called and made an appointment to see this banker and thanks to my old friendship, we got past all the insulating V.P.'s and were ushered directly into the president's office. Despite being a rustic realtor, I compromised my usual dress code and wore a coat and tie for the occasion. John, who wouldn't dress for the Pope, showed up in his usual denim shirt and blue jeans.

Now, despite his imaginative reputation, I just knew

my banker friend was going to hand us the customary loan application form and search for a way to fit John into their pattern. So having made the introduction, I got an inspiration and screwed up the nerve to say, "Arlen, [Smith, Pres of UBank] indulge me for five minutes. I want to tell you the story of what this young fellow has accomplished in the last three years; then you can either usher us out or give him serious consideration. The president indulged me, and I related our foregoing three-year adventure, ending with something like . . . "Why, we could be dealing with the next Donald Trump. I think it could be exciting to see John grow with your bank."

When the banker finally spoke, I was poised to argue tooth and nail with his standard objections, and I'm not sure I hadn't already started to say, "But sir-", when he said, "Fine, we'll make John a $175,000, asset-based loan and to heck with the salary requirements . . . any other questions?"

Now, I learned long ago, when you've made a sale, just say thank you and leave . . . don't beat a dead horse or even a live loan. So we thanked Arlen, picked up our marbles and made a strategic withdrawal. John claims that at the moment of truth he told me to go wait in the car, but that's not true.

However, once again, our synergy had worked; John had produced the track record and I was able to verbalize his story and sell his projected earnings. Now that's a kick! . . . and in the process, I've gained a friend who keeps the game exciting wherein money is just a by-product.

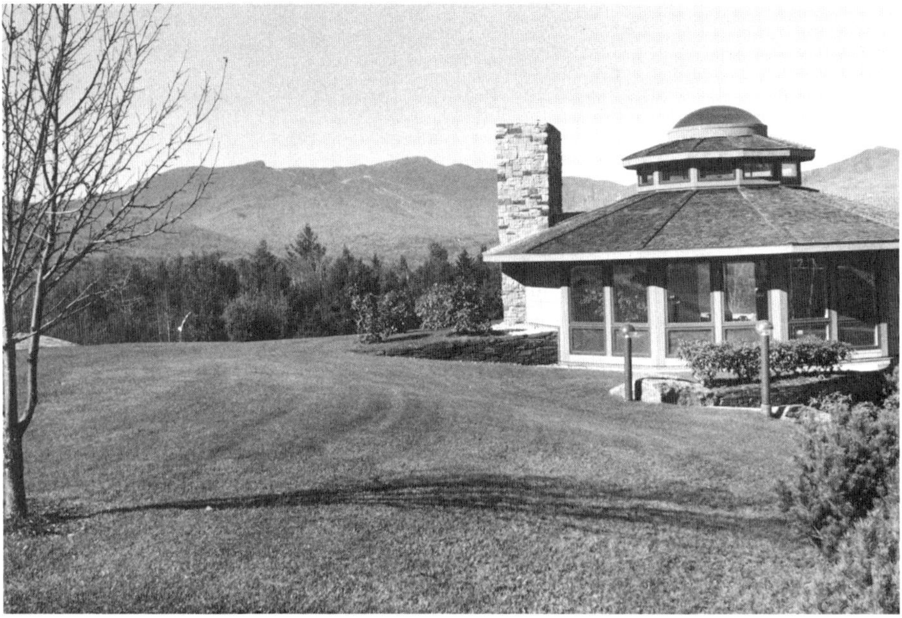

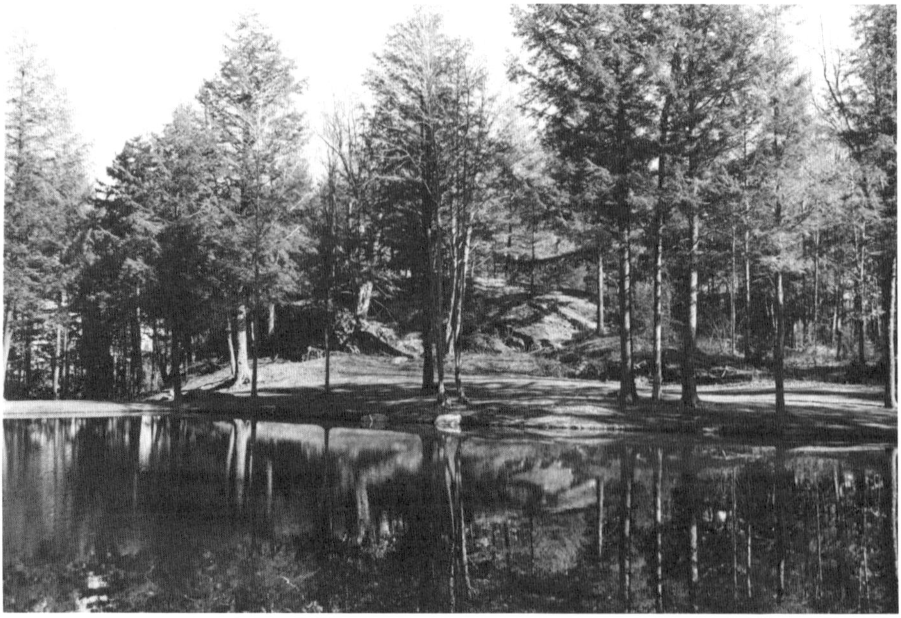

"It's an Ill Wind That Blows No One Some Good"

Chapter 9

My many-faceted friend, Bill Henderson, had built a rather unique and extensive octagonal house at the very crown of Birch Hill in Stowe. Then having made this major expenditure, he realized that his small, two- acre lot was scant protection for a house of that magnitude. So he commissioned me to contact the owner of the 130 acres surrounding him on three sides with the aim of acquiring extra land to "flesh out" his estate. This landowner turned out to be the chief executive of a large management consulting firm serving many of the Fortune 500 companies. In negotiating with this gentleman for Bill's acquisition of six additional acres, I found him alternatively inaccessible, pretentious, and difficult. I felt that he, unaware that I had once been a New York executive myself, treated me like a country bumpkin. Nonetheless, I swallowed my pride, persevered, and worked out Bill's land purchase.

In the process I found, on the acquired 6 acres, an active natural spring from which Bill could create a beautiful, woodland pond. He acted on my suggestion and created a pond which was especially impressive in that it was at the very highest point of Birch Hill, seemingly defying Mother Nature's rule that water seeks its own level.

When the deal was all consummated, I was happy to be free of involvement with the imperious C.E.O. and he was probably equally glad to be free of this niggling little real estate matter midst his demanding schedule. Of course, Bill was delighted with his extra land and his pristine pond.

A year later, the Swanson Estate, at the base of this same Birch Hill, came on the market and Bill was sorely tempted to buy it. This is one of Stowe's most prestigious properties, now worth over $800,000, but when Bill asked my advice, I strongly admonished that he not own two major properties in the same town. The maintenance on each home would be $25,000 a year, and with his holdings elsewhere, he needed a second Stowe domicile like a hole in the head. Nonetheless, the selling broker stressed the advantageous price, the status symbolism, etc., and before I knew it, Bill had made the plunge. When I found the eventual price at which he had acquired the second estate, I found it hard to fault his decision, but Bill said we must now sell his first Birch Hill house. I emphasized that I saw little prospect of a quick sale of his "unique" octagonal house, even with the eight acres and pond.

Then a few months later, I received a call from a fellow realtor asking if I would act, pro-bono, as a intermediary in re-contacting the aforementioned New York C.E.O. on behalf of a lodge owner abutting another part of his 130 acres. This owner of the Gables Inn wanted to buy two abutting acres to his lodge, and also wanted to access the remaining 128 acres for cross- country skiing for his lodge guests.

"No way," I replied to the fellow realtor's request, "he's going to take offense at my bothering him again on a minor matter midst his busy schedule; he's going to talk down his nose to me again, and I'm going to end up saying something I'll regret."

But, finally, after two more calls, she wore down my resistance, and with misgivings, I made the call to New York. Predictably, Ray, the New York executive, first hit me with, "What are you bothering me for?" but finally relented in that he had just bought a new airplane which he could try out by flying up to Vermont.

So it was agreed that I'd meet the new Mitsubishi at the Morristown Airport, Thursday at 9:30 a.m. Over I drove on the appointed morning to meet the luxurious six-seat prop-jet in my three-year-old Datsun. To my dismay I was greeted by my landowner, plus his pilot, plus a business associate, so the cramped quarters of my little Datsun didn't enhance the conviviality of the meeting.

After a somewhat uncomfortable ride, we arrived at the Gables Inn. There I was to find that eight people had just belatedly arrived for their breakfast and the owner was the only available person to accommodate their demands. The owner shunted me aside and said, "Bob, can you stall these people for half-an-hour?"

"IT'S AN ILL WIND THAT BLOWS NO ONE SOME GOOD"

I was flabbergasted. "Sol, at your insistence, this V.I.P. has taken time from his demanding schedule, flown his plane up here at considerable expense, and now you want him and his entourage to cool their heels while you fry eggs? That's crazy!" Nonetheless, he protested that he was up to his elbows in pancakes and scrambled eggs, so I was faced with a quick evasive maneuver or the wrath of God.

Returning to the New York group in the lodge living room, I screwed up my most insouciant smile and blurted out, "Say, Ray, we must drive up and see the wonderful pond Bill Henderson has built on the land you sold him."

"Pond, my ass," he growled, "I didn't fly all the way up here to see some silly pond."

But after much cajoling, he reluctantly and dyspeptically succumbed to getting back in my cramped car and driving to the top of Birch Hill. Ray was a very unhappy camper all the way up the hill. Most providentially, however he was really impacted by the pond's unexpected beauty.

"I've got to admit that is a magnificent setting for a pond," he said. I'm glad you showed it to me and I'm glad I sold Bill the land so he could create it."

Breathing a sigh of relief, I started back to the car for the drive down the hill to the Gables to discuss the two acres and skiing easement with Sol. But as we passed Bill Henderson's octagonal house Ray said offhandedly, "...most unusual structure; I happen to have an octagonal structure on Cape Cod . . . isn't for sale is it?"

"Matter of fact, it is on the market," I replied. "I just happen to have a house key in the car; like to see it?

He's only asking $300,000."

Well, we had walked about ten paces into the house, when this decisive executive turned to me and said, "Tell him I'll take it, but I won't pay a cent over . . . ."

I was speechless . . . a reluctant appointment to help a lodge owner, and eight late breakfast arrivees had just made me about $12,000 in commissions. Of course, between that precipitous offer and the closing of the deal stood many complications, but we got it done, and I chuckle every time I think of those scrambled eggs.

Incidentally, major changes have taken place since Ray bought the house. First, he completely renovated and augmented the structure, further landscaped around the pond, added a satellite rotunda, and opened some of the world's most beautiful views from the crown of land. The place is now an envied showplace, written up in national publications, and Ray, now a friend, is glad for my diversionary tactics.

Trust, What a Wonderful World

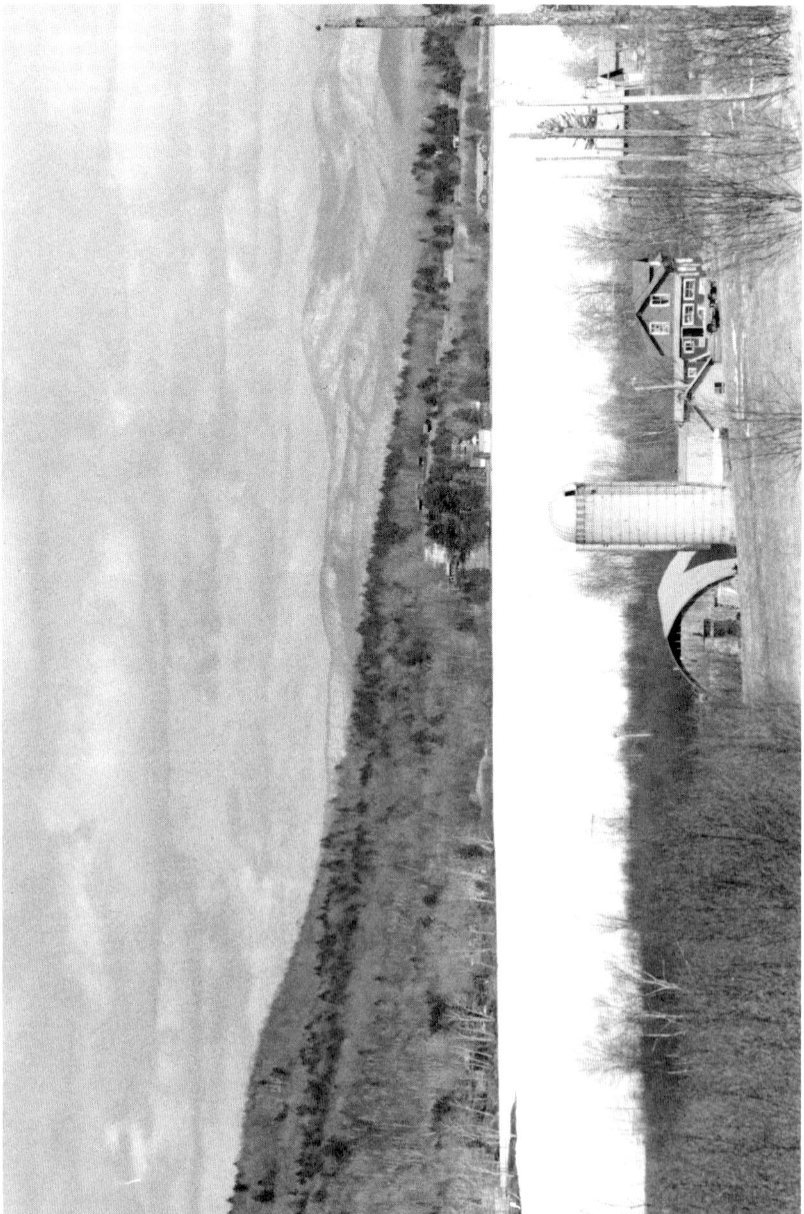

Chapter 10

I walked into our Real Estate office one day, having just returned from my annual visit to England, and overheard Sherry Wilson on the phone.

"You say it's 3.6 acres overlooking Lake Elmore with town road access, spring water, and a hunting camp . . . and the price is $9,500?"

She appeared to get confirmation from the other end of the line, so when she hung up, I said, "If it bears any relation to how it sounds, I'll buy it myself and pay you a commission for answering the phone."

Well, it turned out to be even better than I could have hoped; a parcel of land at the top of a long hill, overlooking the lake, replete with a viable camp building solidly built. A former owner had cut down the trees on the front third of the property leaving an acre of ugly stumps and the woods were quite clotted and ratty, but I knew I'd enjoy the project of thinning the woods and clearing the stumps.

There was only one problem: the three-acre parcel directly below my new land featured rapidly growing poplar trees that would soon obscure the view of the lake. The key to the value and charm of my newly-acquired parcel was the acquisition of that additional piece of land so that I could control and enhance the view.

So I paid a visit to the Lake Elmore Town Clerk and learned that the adjoining piece belonged to a Dr. Kurt Anstreicher of Wilmington, Delaware, who had bought the lot years before in hopes that he or his children would one day build a vacation home thereon. It had eventuated that his sons had moved West and that, getting older, he didn't have the energy or motivation to build a vacation home at this distance. So I called the doctor in Delaware and, after some discussion, I made him an offer commensurate with the price I had paid for the first parcel. He countered with justification for a slightly higher price and we quickly came to agreement on his, still reasonable, price.

I then sent the doctor a proposed contract, delineating terms of 1/3rd down and payment over three years @ 10% interest on the balance; along with reservation for search of the title and verification of the indicated boundaries, etc.

But being a real estate broker, I took special pains to make full disclosure of my motivation for wanting the land, and all of the details of the purchase. Along with the signed proposed agreement, I sent the doctor my check for a token $500.00, agreeing to place 10% of the selling price in his attorney's hand upon receipt of the contract signed and returned by the doctor.

Two weeks later, having no reply from Wilmington, I called the doctor, but was unable to reach him. I made subsequent unsuccessful calls, and finally after 30 days I very disappointedly wrote the doctor assuming he had changed his mind about the sale. Then, after about five weeks from our original verbal agreement I received a call from Dr. Anstreicher. To my voiced assumption that he had changed his mind, he replied with his strong native German accent, "No, ve agreedt und I not go back on dat agreement."

"But Doctor," I protested, "you have my signed contract, and my $500.00; I have nothing!"

To which he replied, "Ve are guht people, ve trust each udder, I send you de papers."

So I hung up, elated that my purchase was still alive, but still uncertain of what the charming old doctor had in mind. I found out one week later when an envelope arrived from Delaware. Enclosed was a "live" deed signed by Dr. Anstreicher, witnessed and notarized. To my astonishment, I now legally owned the property. He had only my $500.00, no signed mortgage note for $8,000, no $4,000 down per our verbal agreement . . . and I held a fully-executed deed to the property.

After years of dealing with all of the protective legal intricacies of real estate transaction . . . and having had only two phone conversations with this gentleman at 800-mile distance, I was stunned that he had the trust in the sound of my voice and the phrasing of my letters to put the land legally in my hands without receiving any substantial payment.

Needless to say, in recording the signed deed and thus taking possession of my new property, I expedited the additional money and signed mortgage note to the doctor; I would have sold body and soul to follow through properly on my agreement. But still at those times when I find myself disappointed in my fellow man, I remember that truly trusting "gentleman" and his act of faith in this real estate broker.

I've asked him to come visit as my guest and see the work I'm doing in beautifying his land . . . I hope he'll get the chance to come . . . I think I'll always consider it to be Dr. Anstreicher's land.

I've since had a reputedly responsible young man ask if he could rent the camp on the property. He's living pretty hand-to-mouth, so I've told him he can't rent it, but he can stay there for free. He has to carry his water from the well and exist on gas lights and a gas fridge, but he's young and those hardships are adventures for the young. I questioned whether I should take the chance of having someone stay at the camp, but then I thought I'll extend the trust to the young man that Dr. Anstreicher extended to me. Things like that do seem to have a ripple effect.

"Now Who's Crazy?"

THE STOWE REPORTER
THURSDAY, NOVEMBER 13, 1969

Editor & Publisher .... D.T. Elliman, Jr.
Associate Editor .... Beverley Willis
Assistant Editor .... Linda Adams

Robert P. Murray
REAL ESTATE

1st on the Mountain Road
244-8595   253-4537   244-8017

1100 Acres, spectacular views, 30 miles from Stowe, streams, road frontage, good house, barn..........................$180,000.oo.

Large farms near Rt. 100-Vt. 89 intersection, reasonable prices.

200 acre farm, 3 miles from Stowe Village..........$110,000.oo.

300 acre farm, stocked & tooled, ties 70 cows, 150 acre tillage, house excellent condition.......................$110,000.oo.

Farms & land right to the border.

Chapter 11

I guess we all seek to be liked by our neighbors and friends. To some of us, life is one long popularity contest. But trying to please everyone can be an exhausting process, and as we mature, most of us realize that some people are just going to have a natural antipathy for our particular type . . . and that's O.K.

When I first knew Jim Jackson he was one of those people who just didn't like the cut of my jib. Unfortunately for me, he happened to be looking for a large tract of land at that time, and his Greenwich, Conn. background definitely equipped him with the wherewithal to make a substantial investment. Though I was then probably the foremost authority on land in the area, I resigned myself not to be in the ballgame where Jim was concerned.

Then one day I was eating at the counter at Giroux's Restaurant (which was the equivalent of the floor of the New York Stock Exchange where Stowe real estate was concerned), when Ted McKay jabbed me unceremoniously on the shoulder to say, "You gotta come over here and talk with Jackson; he's looking for a special piece of development land and you're the guy who can find it for him."

Jim still wasn't putting forth a very cordial hand, but "necessity is the mother of strange bedfellows" (and mixed metaphors), so we set about looking for the ideal 100 acres. Jim wanted views, easy access, receptive soils, location, meadows, forest, etc. It was a lot of criteria, and for a while I struck out in trying to fill Jim's bill.

Then I got wind of an approximate 130 acre parcel in the northern part of Stowe that seemed to embody all of Jim's needs. When I enquired about the property, however, I was generally dissuaded from pursuing the situation as the owner had just been discharged from the Vermont State Mental Institution after an eleven-year stay. He was generally assumed incompetent to enter into any fruitful negotiation. I guess the reason this unique parcel of land had remained untouched was this very assumption, by all concerned, that the man was not competent of being approached.

But I figured the worst he could do was throw me out on my ear, so I looked up Mr. Harold Bedell and knocked on his door. As predicted, he was quite reticent at first, but finally he invited me in and we ended up in a long conversation. He was very open about his previous hospitalization, but insisted that his family had misinterpreted his, high-strung personality and had mistakenly committed him. Frankly, from the gist of our long conversation, I felt prone to concur and the longer I knew the man, the more convinced I became that his commitment had been unnecessary. He didn't march to the normal drummer, but he was colorful and enthusiastic, and I came to enjoy and like the man.

In regard to the land he said, "First, let me show it to you and then we can talk some more."

Now, seeing the land turned out to be a strenuous and intrepid exercise. I was positioned standing on the back of his tractor, and we drove through a very steep, wooded terrain. I fell off a couple of times, but when we reached the height of the land, I felt duly rewarded. There, interspersed with lovely wooded copses and glades, were four separate meadow areas. Actually Harold had planted potatoes in one meadow and sunflowers in another, but the combination of high meadows and woods, offering stunning views of the Mansfield range, created a beautiful mosaic.

Then, after another harrowing tractor ride back down the hill, Harold said, "I like you young fellow and you really appreciate my land, so I'm going to let you handle it. I'm getting on in years and it's time for me to pleasure myself with a better car and a fishing boat, so you get me a fair price and we'll do business."

I, quite candidly, told Mr. Bedell that I might have a buyer who would be perfect for his land, so we put a substantial price on the property, signed the listing and I went off in search of Jim Jackson.

After Jim and I had walked the land thoroughly, studied aerial photos, and checked out the soils, there was little doubt that he wanted the property. The only reservation was whether or not the cost of building an access road up that hill would be prohibitive. But once he'd designed a serpentine drive up the hill and recieved a couple of competitive bids, Jim signed the contract that promised a solid price (for those days) to Mr. Bedell.

I must admit that, between signing and closing, I had some uneasy moments worrying about this septuagenarian's motor jaunts to N.Y. State to call on a lady he'd met. And I couldn't help feeling guilty that I may have been more concerned about my projected closing than I was about Harold's life and limb. I even considered offering to be his chauffeur, rejecting the idea as being transparent. Sure enough, however, everyone was finally ushered into the lawyer's office for the closing 30 days hence. Although dwarfed by escalating real estate prices since, the closing check was, to that date, the largest ever paid for a parcel of land in Stowe, and as he picked up his check, Harold turned to the assembled group and calmly said, "Now who's crazy?"

I wanted to applaud the old gentleman. Now, he could spend his waning years enjoying his new car and fishing on his new boat (with his new lady), and perhaps it would help make up for the eleven wasted years.

There is a P.S. to the story. I hadn't forgotten that Ted McKay had initiated the whole deal that day at Giroux Restaurant, so I sought him out at his current building site. I found him on the roof, shingling.

"Ted, come down here; I've got to talk with you," I called.

I got the expected terse profane reply, for which Ted was so famous, to the effect, "Screw you, I'm busy." But

I persisted and he finally, impatiently, climbed down to ask, "Now what's the big deal?"

"The big deal is I owe you a debt of gratitude, so here's a check for $1,000. The law won't let me give you a finder's fee so let's just call this happy birthday in advance."

The gesture was a total surprise for Ted, who had many uses for the largess, and I must say, I've never gotten more fun out of spending $1,000.

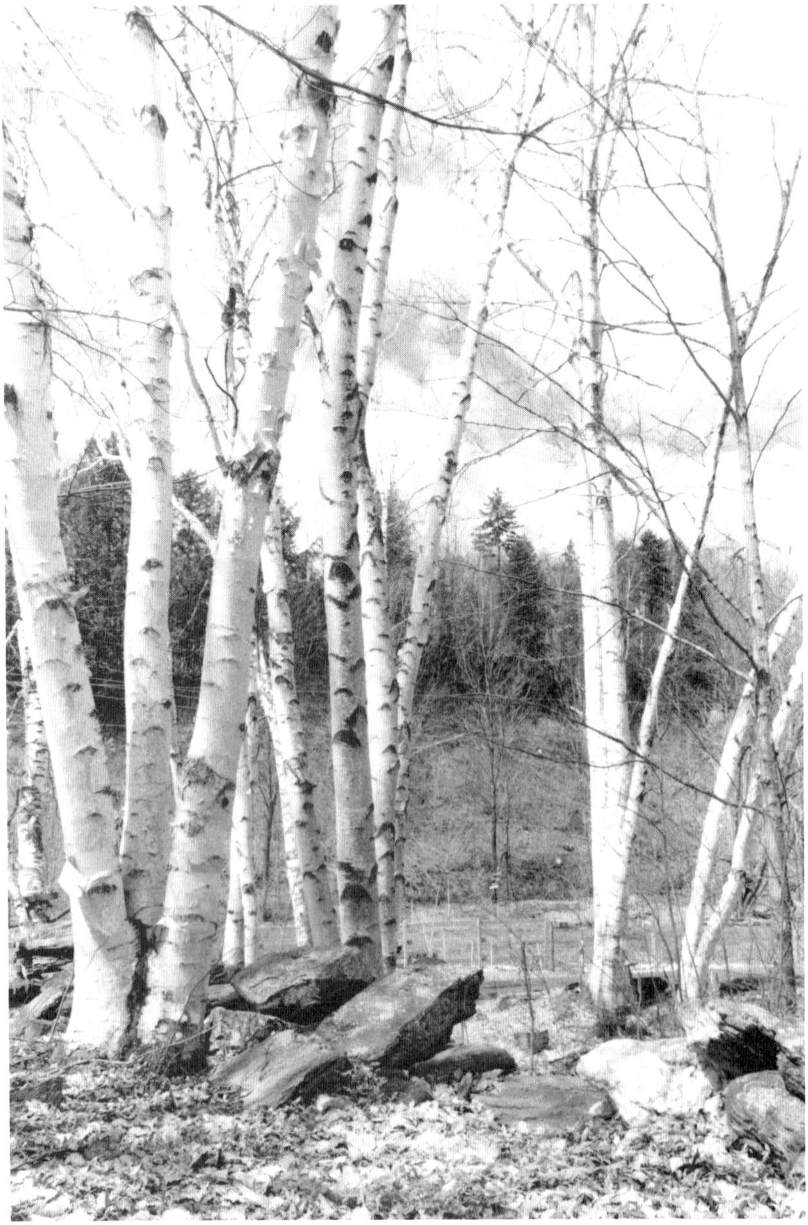

"A Nest of Robins in Its Hair"

Chapter 12

Despite claims to the contrary by the creationist-fundamentalist Christians, there seems to be a wide acceptance that we humans did evolve from the ape kingdom... and there seems to be a vestigial throw-back aspect of my make-up that has a fascination with climbing trees. For instance, in the process of opening up views from some of my land in Sterling Valley, I climbed seventy-foot giants with my trusty chain saw to cut the top 15 feet off those imposing arboreal behemoths in the most dangerous exercise I've yet undertaken in the woods. In retrospect, without professional equipment, I was lucky to come away with both arms and both legs.

A more sane exercise of my tree-climbing proclivities has been the scaling of trees to confirm view potential from parcels of land under consideration by real estate customers. Deep in the forest, it's hard to tell what views can be achieved by clearing a building site or selectively trimming trees. By the nature of the terrain, the degree of descent of the land, and a general knowledge of the area, I can pretty closely predict the views that can be achieved by clearing a site in the forest: but when a customer is on the verge of making an important commitment, he often wants more evidence than conjecture. I can still remember Frank Jouannet shouting to me, "Come down out of that damned tree before you break your neck... I'll sign the contract!"

Perhaps my most effective ascent was climbing the tallest tree at the apex of Birch Hill. I had determined, by studying aerial maps, that if the Birch Hill complex were combined with the Cady Hill complex rising up from the opposite River Road side of the mountain, there could, potentially, be access into both areas from the Mountain Road in Stowe. That would give residents a hypotenuse route South, skirting the congestion of Stowe Village and the Rt. 100 intersection.

However, I couldn't determine from the aerial photo how the terrains of these large abutting land parcels would mesh, as far as road feasibility was concerned, short of very expensive topographical surveying or the hiring of a helicopter. But once I had climbed about 75 ft. up the tallest pine at the apex of elevation, the lay of the land with its pitches, slopes, benches, and plateaus became quite apparent. In a meeting with the Birch Hill developers, I was able to say with conviction that the "northwest passage" through Birch Hill/Cady Hill was a very practical option, and as a result was able to convince them to acquire this 200-acre tract of valuable land.

In a less practical and more aesthetic episode, I savor the memory of the late September night when a strong wind was scattering white clouds across the face of a full moon. I was awakened at 2 am by the rustle of lilac branches being blown against my little farmhouse window. *It was as if Mother Nature was calling me out to play, and view her tempestuous splendor.*

In an almost hypnotic state, I arose from my bed, wandered outside into the moonlight, climed high into a crotch of a nearby beech tree, and there basked in the elemental sensuality of the wind beating against my body, the moon shining on my face and the tree swaying under my feet, It was like those once rare magic moments at sea, on the flying bridge of our Navy destroyer, underway at full speed on a warm moonlight night.

If you enjoy the privacy that Vermont often affords, and are, thus not concerned about being reported for lunacy by well-meaning neighbors, then I recommend when the wind and the moon are right and Mother Nature taps on your window, that you get up and follow her lead.

Characteristically, after I read Robert Frost's essay on "Swinging Birches," I couldn't resist testing whether this colorful activity actually worked. It does . . . and although not as glamorous or exhilarating as hang-gliding or sky-diving, it does constitute one of nature's natural thrills. To indulge in the sport, one must first seek out the right size birch. It shouldn't be more than 18 inches in diameter at its base and it shouldn't be more than 27 feet high, and it must have enough accessible small branches that one can readily climb to the top. Late spring and summer are the optimum times when the birch is most vigorous and flexible.

Then one climbs to the top of the tree where the weight of your body will start the birch swinging precariously. At that critical moment, you invert the grip of your two hands around the top of the trunk and just step out into space. If you've chosen and calculated correctly, you'll then enjoy a wonderful and gentle ride to the ground. In season, it's highly unlikely that the birch will snap for it's an extremely flexible tree as you can observe in bowed birches after a windstorm. The only one that ever broke under me still let me down with minimal impact.

The closest I ever came to injury was through selection of a birch too large for the purpose. After I swung out, I found myself hanging about 15 feet from the ground with insufficient weight to bend the birch all the way. I hung there quite helpless, unable to climb back up and faced with a broken ankle if I let go. Fortunately, I was accompanied by John Meaker, a very athletic and intrepid fellow, who, assessing the situation in an instant, clambered up the tree and climbed out to add his weight to mine, whence the tree gently deposited us both on terra firma. It happened during the birch- swinging portion of my annual outdoor party, so John got a big round of applause.

My most surprising birch experience began at a rather formal dinner party on Tabor Hill. Amongst the guests was a handsome young S.A.C. pilot; one of those fighter pilots on the U.S.A.'s first line of defense, who scramble at 700 miles per hour to meet any incoming threat by foreign forces. I was most impressed by this young aviator and his breast full of decorations. How the conversation got around to Vermontiana, Robert Frost and birch swinging, I don't know, but I guess I observed that in my simple earth-bound world, I found it quite a kick.

Almost like a knee-jerk reflex this intrepid fellow said, "I want to try it."

Despite my protestations that it would all be very pedestrian compared to his exciting vocation, he soon had me up from the table and out in the lane selecting the right size birches. We proceeded to climb neighboring birches about 25 feet in height, at which point he said, "Do you mean we now just step out in space and trust these fragile trees?"

"Yeah," I replied, "but you do much more dangerous things every day of your life."

Still clinging to the birch, he said, "But I could break my ankle and be out of commission."

I must say, I was surprised at his reaction; we weren't 25,000 feet from the ground, we were only 25 feet up. But I guess it was a new unknown to him, and he'd have a tough time explaining to his commanding officer that he was hors-de-combat from swinging birches.

At any rate, I finally threw caution to the wind and stepped out into the abyss for a lovely ride to the ground, with the pilot following suit.

"Wow, that was terrific!" came his comment.

As I might have guessed, having done it once, he wanted to swing every birch on the property. I really had a tough time getting him to rejoin our hostess and the dinner party. It did, however, confirm my conviction that, even for fly boys, birch swinging can be a unique thrill. I should add the caveat not to let my fascination with trees lead you down the proverbial garden path. Keep in mind the story of the tree surgeon who was fatally injured falling out of a patient. Enjoy the experience if you are so moved, but remember, tree climbing and tree swinging aren't for everyone.

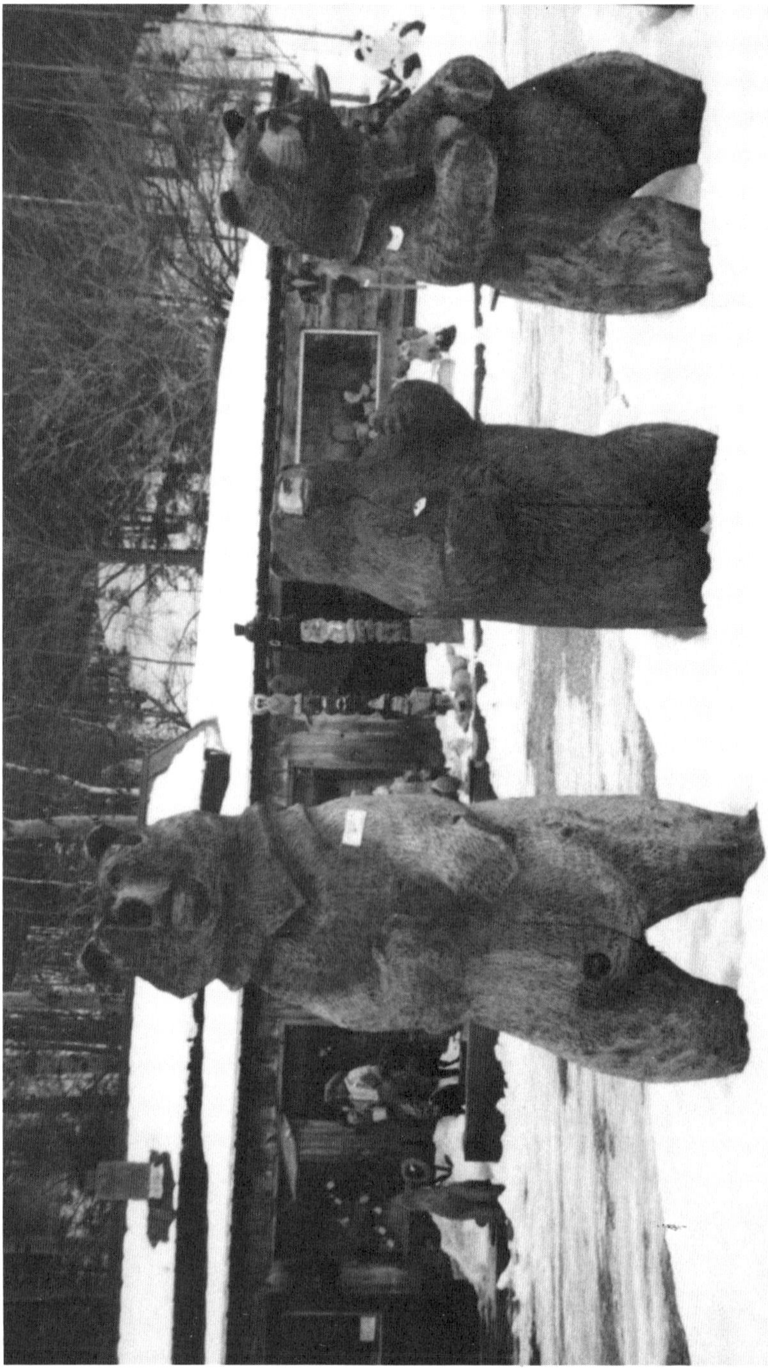

"Them and Us"

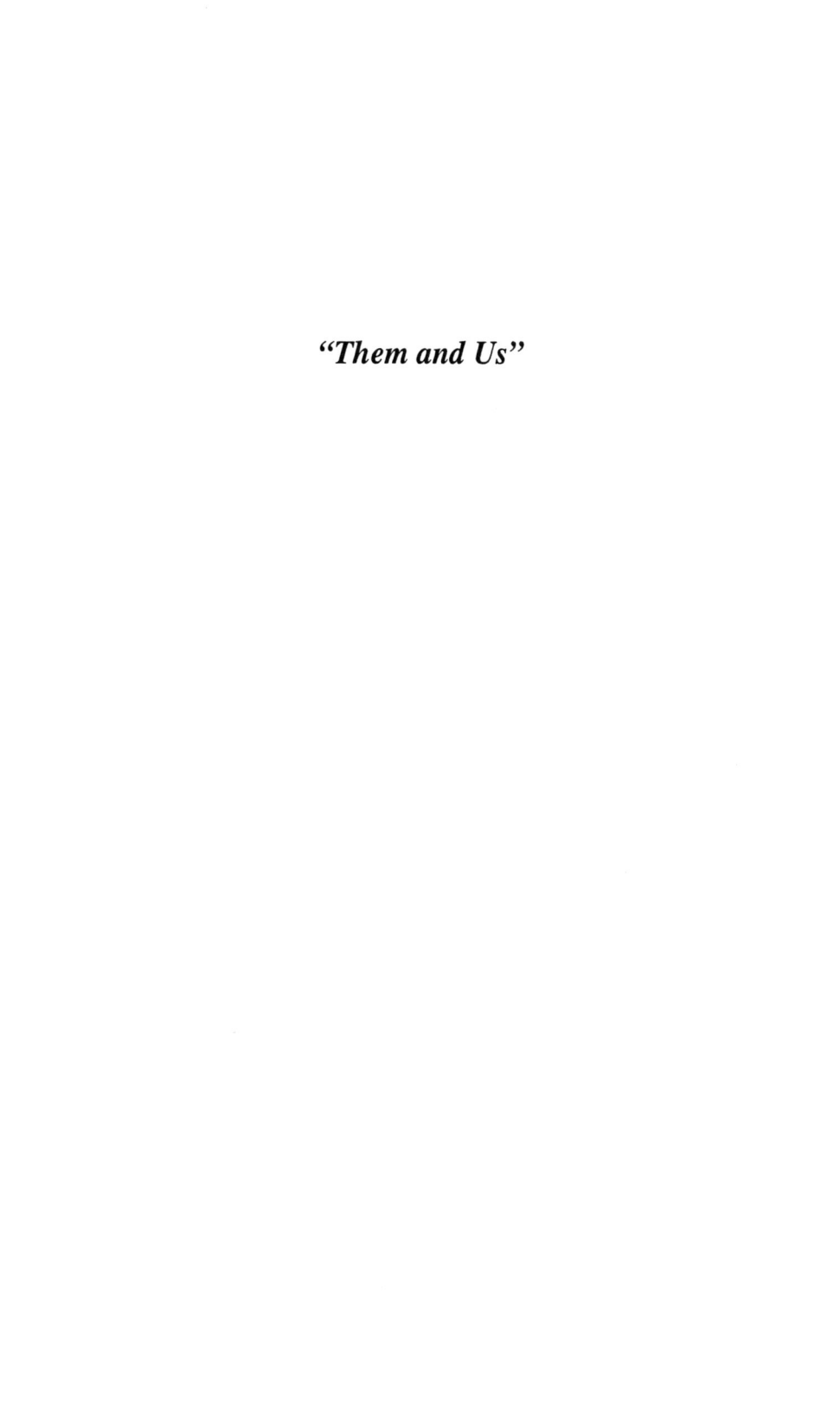

Chapter 13

"Them and Us"

The surest way to become a Vermonter is to be born here; other routes are much less certain. My 32 years as a Vermont resident accords me Vermont status when I'm visiting other places, but among native Vermonters, I'm still somewhat of a "downcountry flatlander". For example, the young man who rebuilt my little barn last year happens to be 27 years old. He was born here and has spent those 27 years in Vermont. He's definitely a Vermonter. I, on the other hand, arrived in Vermont five years before he was born, but my status is somewhat more questionable.

The natives and the nouveaus share a great deal in Vermont like town governments and school boards, etc., but there are inviolable areas where it seems "never the twain shall meet." One such area is skiing. Although downhill skiing started here in the late 1930's, it was introduced to the Green Mountains by out-of-staters, and early-on, skiing was a very elitist sport. My first ski flight to the Alps included Dedo Dupont, of Delaware, Tom Watson of IBM, etc. In early years at Stowe, Dina

Merrill stayed at the Foster Place, the Ali Kahn stayed at Ten Acres, Ella Raines stayed at the Topnotch, and the Kennedys stayed at the Lodge. Although skiing, in recent years, has become a much more egalitarian activity, along with golf and other formerly restricted pastimes, many Vermonters still consider it a superimposition on Vermont from the outside and a "darned-fool" waste of time.

Native Vermonters instead have espoused snowmobiling as their "thing." It figures, 'cause most Vermonters love to tinker with machinery. I think that evolves from the fact that, to survive, the farmer has to have a natural grasp of the working of machinery and the ability to deal with frequent breakdowns. If he had to hire a repairman to come out to his farm every time a minor glitch developed in the working of his tractor or baler he'd go broke. So when the snowmobile came along, it was right up his alley, or furrow, as the case may be. He could get his fresh air, cover Vermont's terrain on a mechanical device as is his wont, and have a wonderful new internal combustion engine with which to tinker, trade or auction.

In many other ways, the native Vermonter feels separate, and maybe at least subconsciously resentful of all these yuppies, environmentalists, and pseudo-intellectuals who have invaded his state and instituted liberal politics, ecological laws, and the welfare state. For instance, since resident students can choose to vote in Vermont, and the city of Burlington encompasses five institutions of higher learning, our largest city now has a socialist government and a recent mayor from Brooklyn, a situation never conceived of in the old days of solid, conservative Vermont.

On the other hand, because even displaced city kids realize that the Vermont farm is the backbone of our environmental beauty as well as our economy, there has been accommodation by both groups to one another. I happen to think that the institution of the Vermont town meeting, America's oldest form of true democracy, has helped to ease the friction between "them and us." On that one hallowed day a year, every person has one vote, every person is equal, and every person can stand up to say his or her piece and vent their spleen.

Perhaps a good example of the co-existence between "them and us" has been my relationship with Milo and Emma Marshall, my Gregg Hill neighbors. The Marshalls owned a large farm on Gregg Hill for generations. Although Uncle Dan Marshall migrated to the city and became professor at Tufts University, most of the Marshalls have stayed or gravitated back to the home place in Waterbury Center, Vermont. Milo doesn't boast a degree from an Ivy League College, but when it comes to such disparate areas as mechanics and finance he has instinctive intelligence I find hard to match.

I first met him when he drove up in his pick-up to observe my efforts to rebuild my old farmhouse. He probably thought I'd have been smarter to tear down the tired old structure and start from scratch. He already knew I was a bachelor because he later told me he expected a lot more action when he first saw me drive up the road in a yellow mustang convertible with a guitar protruding from the back seat.

But when he stopped by that first day, he didn't say a word for a while . . . then he simply said, "Looks like you're doin' quite a job on that house . . . but it seems like you got the cage before you got the bird." Pretty darn incisive commentary, and more farseeing, as it turns out, than I might have hoped.

In recent years, Milo has phased out of the earth-moving/road building business into more artistically creative endeavors. After an effort to make and market antique spinning wheel replicas died aborning, because the public would not meet the high cost of producing this delicate product, Milo developed a most unlikely alternative . . . chain saw sculpture.

He combined his natural creative flare with twenty years of wielding a chain saw in clearing rights-of-way through the woods during his road-building years. Milo found he could fine-tune the use of the cumbersome chain saw to create bears out of tree trunks, and has since turned out all manner of wildlife sculpture. People come from hundreds of miles away to buy Milo's bears and his work is now in 43 of the 50 states.

Marveling at his ability to create detail with these cumbersome and dangerous machine tools, a newspaper reporter interviewing Milo asked how he knew where and when to cut. With the soul of brevity, he replied, "you just strip the bark off the tree trunk, and then you cut away everything that isn't bear."

Now, I realize that Rodin wasn't such a genius after all

. . . he merely took a block of granite, his hammer and his chisel, and then cut away everything that wasn't "Thinker."

Over the years, Milo and I have enjoyed a synergistic relationship (he says I could talk plainer than that). I've been able to advise him on buying and selling some of his real estate; he's been able to help me estimate earth-moving jobs, help me access some acrobatic building sites, and put me in touch with potential real estate clients.

When a major water pipe burst in my house while I was away, it was Milo who was on the scene to help salvage a tragic situation, and insist on taking me in 'til we got the place livable.

Still there are areas we don't share. I don't know why, at times, he insists on using double negatives when he's had as many years of English as I; he counters that if he used the pretentious verbiage I throw around, nobody'd know what he was talking about.

I like Pavoratti; he likes Willie Nelson. (Actually, I think Willie Nelson is one of the great creative talents of our time, but I'd never let Milo know.)

I usually eat supper about 8:00 p.m.; Milo and Emma sit down about 5:45. The Marshalls definitely don't eat quiche, and as Professor Frank Bryan says, they sure as hell don't milk goats.

Yet I cherish the bridging of the gap. Truer, kinder, more honest friends never existed than the Marshalls, and as the years pass, our differences blur. I'm beginning to look askance at those pseudo-pretentious liberals that I see invading Vermont . . . "Come up here to look down their noses and tell us how to run our state."

My gosh, maybe I'm starting to become a real Vermonter myself. Soon I'll be talking about the "wicked good views" from my farm, or telling my neighbors that "I heard their dog turned up missing." Why, as I sit here at my typewriter, I may already be evolving into an "us."

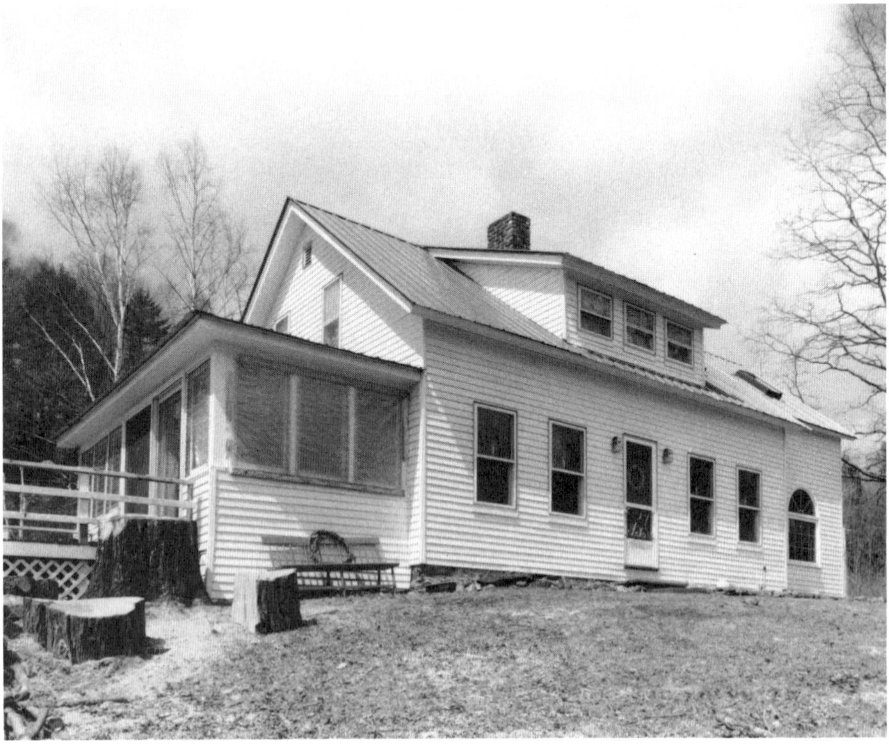

"A Tough New York Female"

"A TOUGH NEW YORK FEMALE"

CHAPTER 14

When George Bernard Shaw wrote "Man and Superman" he knew from whence he spoke. "Sugar and spice and everything nice" often covers a core of steel. In my real estate experience, the so-called "weaker sex" is often much more demanding and difficult to placate or satisfy than the male of the species.

When Syd and Abbie Weinstein dissolved their marriage, Abbie ended up with a lovely old farmhouse and 38 acres in Waterbury Center, VT. As Abbie had a growing business in Port Chester N.Y. and a new man in her life, she decided to sell the Vermont property.

Now Abbie, albeit charming, is a successful, assertive, athletic, no-nonsense lady . . . and she set a firm price on her property. Problem was, activity was slow that year, and we just couldn't come up with the buyer who could afford the house, barn and all 38 acres.

After frustrated efforts to market the property, I got a brainstorm . . . if Abbie would allow me to soil-test and spin off 12 of the acres at the far end of the property, we might be able to realize a big enough price that she could afford to lower the price on the house, barn, and remaining 26 acres.

The catch was that the 12 acres was a clotted mess of virtually impenetrable woods. "No problem," I said, "I love to work with Mother Nature; two weeks with my chain saw, limber, and axe and I'll have it looking like the Bois Du Bologne."

"Murray, if you want to put forth all that effort gratis, with no recompense until, if, and when you sell the property, be my guest," replied Abbie.

So, loving the woods, I went to work, and in no time by thinning it out, trimming off the lower branches of the larger trees, and clearing the forest floor of years of accumulation, I'd let the natural beauty of the parcel show through.

Then, sure enough, another two weeks later, we'd sold the twelve acres to a couple of young landscape architects from Connecticut who fell in love with the land.

Shortly thereafter, the perfect young couple came along who could afford the house and remaining 26 acres at the commensurately-adjusted price and we'd managed to realize more than the original total asking price demanded by Abbie.

Abbie came up to Waterbury for the closing on the house, and after the details had finally been worked out at the attorney's office, she turned to me and said, "Well, Murray, you've managed to make two commissions; one on the twelve acres and another on the house, so we expect you to take us all to dinner tonight at an up-scale restaurant . . . and I think that should include the Cahills, (the buyer's) Mrs. St. Louis (former owner), Attorney Nancy Green, co-broker Michelle Smith, et. al."

With six for dinner, I could see my modest commission fast dwindling, but I bravely agreed that I would be happy to take all involved to a "first-class" restaurant. So it was settled that we'd all meet at the Villa Tragara at 8:00 p.m. that evening with appropriate emphasis that I bring my checkbook.

I arrived at the Villa Tragara punctually at 8:00 p.m., and was surprised to find that the assembled group was already there and seated. I felt my coat pocket to make sure the checkbook was there, as I mentally multiplied $35.00 by six. But as I took my place, I was stunned to find a gift-wrapped box and one of the loveliest letters I've ever received. The box held a beautiful watch and the letter included words to the effect that "we couldn't have pulled it off without your efforts above and beyond, etc."

Turned out that the dinner was pre-paid and that my "tough" New York lady was one of the kindest, most generous people I've ever dealt with. That's what renews one's faith and makes all the effort worthwhile.

"Development on a Micro-Scale"

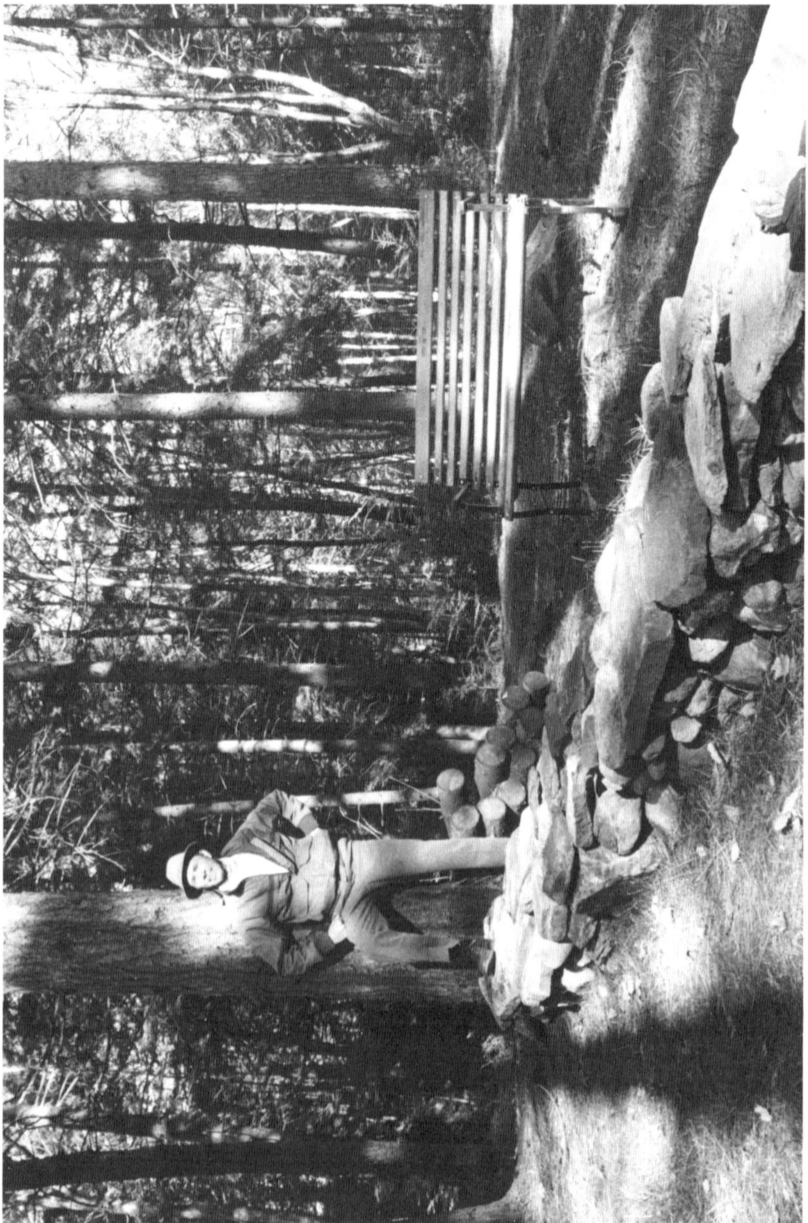

Chapter 15

Conservationism, the preservation of our environment is definitely the "zeit geist" of our times. Faced with burgeoning world population* and industrialization, the concern over the contamination of our land, air and water is well justified. And there's a growing interdependence; what I do to pollute and foul my own nest increasingly affects my neighbor, my state, and my nation.

Vermont, however, seems to be the destination of more than its share of young idealists who have come to save us from ourselves. Having organized a state-wide group called "Balanced View" which sought to save our precious natural environment in Vermont without destroying our economy in the process, I've been involved with both sides of the environmental issue.

In that regard, one of the gratifying things about Vermont is that we have truly representative government, responsive through the Town Meeting process, and an

---

* The present net increase in world population is now at the rate of one new human being every 3 seconds.

amazingly accessible legislature. On my first visit to the legislature, I entered through the massive door, into the rotunda of the state capitol, hat in hand, feeling very small and inadequate. Almost immediately a passing legislator said, "Bob Murray, what the heck brings you to the midst of our deliberations?" I was soon to be reminded that we still have only 500,000 souls in this state, and if you have a legitimate point of view on any issue, you can be heard.

Nonetheless, a prospective developer has a very forbidding gauntlet of local, regional, and state regulations to run before he can ever sink a blade in the earth . . . compounding the cost in interest, engineering, attorneys, etc., caused by the long delays of the process. If a project is to be solvent, these costs must eventually be borne by the consumer, so affordable housing often suffers.

Fortunately for me, my kind of development is on a very elemental scale. It's my joy to take one piece of five or ten acres at a time (preferably the most unkempt woodlot) and develop this "ugly duckling" into a swan or a virtual park. It's sort of gardening on a grand scale, and I figure it's also a reversion to the primordial hunter-gatherer stage of human evolution. It's very hard to worry about anything when you're working in the woods, and it has the most healing effect on the mind and soul after a day of negotiation or conflict in the real estate business.

Personally, my benefits are four-fold:
I get my daily physical exercise;

I accumulate my annual firewood, piece by piece;
I beautify and enhance the value of the land on
   which I'm working; and
I experience the ineffable joy of communing
   with nature in an active,
   constructive process.

I find that the pleasure of ownership quickly cloys, whereas the joy of working with the land is a growing thing.

My current project, for instance, which I've dubbed "Murray Memorial Park II" is five acres in a prestigious section of Stowe. It came into my possession in an unusual way. A favorite client of mine, who was developing a 70-acre parcel in the Week's Hill area, had gotten caught in the high-interest, high-regulation squeeze of 1978 and needed $10,000 to stave off bank foreclosure. At that point in my life I had, quite coincidentally, accumulated exactly $10,000 in my bank account. I counted this guy as a real friend, and saying to myself, "What are friends for?" I blithely drew a check for the $10,000 to this developer friend.

At first he strongly resisted my gesture; then he said he'd accept the check only if I'd accept a deed for the corner lot of the subdivision in consideration. And so, I acquired a very strategic piece of land, with great growth potential, which also just happened to be crying out for some tender loving care.

Perhaps it's akin to the love we lavish on a stray dog who needs T.L.C., food and grooming; but there is a special joy in taking a tangled mess of woods and making it beautiful. To quote Ogden Nash's paraphrase of Joyce Kilmer, "I think that I shall never see a billboard lovely as a tree."

In this beautification process, it helps to understand that in every forest there is a competition or battle for survival going on for the available sunlight and nutrients from the soil. This is particularly fascinating to observe in Vermont where we have the complete gamut of hardwood and softwood trees: beech, birch, maple, pine, spruce, oak, hemlock, basswood, etc. Of course, these are not sixty-minute competitions like in the N.F.L. It may take ten years to determine the winner, but the contest between stands and individual trees still quietly goes on.

One of the reasons that New England has remained so green and forested is that when a blight or disease temporarily decimates a particular species of tree, there is such a wide variety of other species to replace the fallen victims that the forest as a whole survives. We are at present suffering a beech blight which infects the trunks of these stately giants and causes them to self-destruct. However, when almost all of the beech have died and disappeared from Vermont's forests, the host or milieu of the disease will be minimized and the disease with it. Then the remaining young saplings will begin the long road back to re-establishing the breed. You can observe this phenomenon in the woods right now as the tiny beech saplings are beginning to re-assert themselves.

When I acquired "Memorial Park II," it had three distinct areas within the 5.2 acres all crying out for management.

The first area consisted of two acres of sugar maples next to Weeks Hill Road. These maples were thriving and winning the competition with the ironwood trees in their midst, but the myriad maple saplings needed thinning to reduce competition for the available nutrients with the more mature specimens. Eventually, the saplings would have been choked out by their more pervasive brothers, but my pruning accelerated the process of creating a secluded maple grove.

The second area was along the lower section of the property near the confluence of the brooks where a combination of moist soil and large boulders provide the yellow birch both the dampness and the anchors their root structure seems to seek. Birch, incidently, is a rather unique species in that it grows in several forms: i.e., the grey birch which is a soft wood and virtually a weed tree; the white birch which, while decorative, is still a less than hard wood with shallow root structure; and the yellow birch which is hard and hardy with anchoring root structure. The yellow birch is obviously the more valuable and useful of the three.

The third area, or center core of the five-acre property, had started out, perhaps twenty-five years before, with thousands of young hemlock and red pine. Over the years, most of the red pine had managed to grow faster and taller than the hemlock, thus creating a canopy over the hemlock. As a result, the hemlock and lesser pines became deprived of the available sunlight and grew small

"DEVELOPMENT ON A MICRO-SCALE"

and spavined compared with the successful red pines reaching for the light. Thus when the land came to me, there were magnificent 70-foot pine trees above a clotted mess of stunted and dying pines and hemlock. So much of this lower growth was dead or dying that one could hardly walk thru the woods without having to clamber over crisscrossed trunks . . . and one hardly noticed the stately pines above because of the obscuring of the slash below. So my initial project was to remove all this lower growth including some misbegotten gnarled hemlocks which were still competing with the stately red pine plantation.

Of course, because of the volume of this dross or slash, I had to establish a few strategic burning locations where the refuse could be burned without endangering other trees. Now, naturally, burning amid the woods requires great care; one mistake can start a conflagration that would leave the beloved woods looking like Hiroshima after the A-bomb. With all the dead "slash" undergrowth, this project called for particular care.

The first night of burning I had raked an area clear, dug a little perimeter ditch and carefully started the burning process, but I hadn't counted on the smoldering of the peat-like undergrowth. The next day when I returned to the site, I found some smoke still rising from the ashes. I heard footsteps behind me and turned to find the imposing figure of the Stowe Fire Marshall looming. He checked out my burning permit, and then made the following pronouncement.

"I think you're seeing the evidence that a fire may not

be out when you think it is. Now I'm not going to bug you and look down the back of your neck, but I live right down the road, and if you set fire to these woods, you'd best head straight for Mexico; 'do not pass go; do not collect $200.' *Now handle with care!"*

I quickly got the message, and I also got an inkling of why northern Vermont has not had a major forest fire since 1929.

At any rate, "Murray Memorial Park" now has a stone-pillared entry way, three beautiful interior stone walls, two park benches, interspersed greenswards 'neath stately 70-foot pines, wading pools in the stream, a pristine maple grove, and a cleared view to the meadows beyond.

In the process, I've had to remove some ugly old hemlocks that made the earth shake when they were felled. In achieving views, I've:

- scaled up and topped tall trees with a chain saw at considerable danger to life and limb.

- climbed up "hung-up" pine trees, detached and ridden them to the ground.

- incurred many nicks, cuts, burns, and small wounds while still keeping all my fingers and toes.

Some days I've left the woods so tired, I could hardly make it to the car; and yet I've enjoyed every minute I've spent on that land.

It's been like creating a large landscape mural . . . not

on canvas, but on the face of Mother Nature herself. Now I know for sure that it's only in working with a possession or a relationship that makes it truly joyful. I recommend that everyone get themselves a piece of land or a garden plot and learn the joys of working with nature.

And remember this is one area of our modern life where efficiency spoils the whole process. It's a unique area where we can escape the despotism of time and not have to fill "the unforgiving minute with 60 seconds worth of distance run."

The other thing my woods experience has shown me is the importance of having a daily activity that gives both gratification and a sense of accomplishment. It's great to wake up in the morning looking forward to some gratifying activity. For me neither fast cars nor spectator sports do the trick . . . working with my beloved woods and then stepping back and appraising the beauty I've created in cooperation with God . . . that's truly fulfilling.

"Rights of Way"

Chapter 16

If one is selling real estate in a city or in suburbia, rights-of-way may not require a great deal of attention, but in rural Vermont one had better be sure they are clearly defined and properly deeded. There is a general law in Vermont that people cannot be denied access to their land, but often that access is only for logging or agricultural purposes, and does not include vehicular traffic. One could, unwittingly, buy a beautiful Shangri-La meadow and subsequently find that it is effectively land-locked.

One such case was in connection with the Covered Bridge Development in Stowe, across the West Branch from the Topnotch. Bill Murphy bought 66 acres of valuable land only to find on a second search of the title that a sliver of land, encompassing less than a quarter of an acre, cut across the only access. This threatened to effectively frustrate the development of the property.

When we discovered the situation, I called Mrs. Gloria McLane in New Jersey (the heir to the old Houston Place that lies adjacent across the river) to explain our dilemma. I explained that she held title to the "sliver" and cited the metes and bounds and deed references from the Town Records. Mrs. McLane found it hard to grasp what I was trying to convey over the phone, and sounded reluctant to help us solve our problem without extended legal consultation.

However, my friend Bill took the bull by the horns and suggested the following. First, I was to call Mr. and Mrs. McLane and invite them to dinner at the "Top of the Sixes" in New York City. Second, I was to create an overlay map which was to show the property with its historical accretions along with a superimposition of the "McLane Sliver" as it cut across the access. Third, I was to have a quit-claim deed drawn up relinquishing claim to the "sliver" by the McLanes.

Having accomplished all of this in a couple of days, I then flew to New York and met the Murphys and the McLanes atop "The Sixes." We had a lovely dinner, learned a lot of history of the old Houston property, presented our problem and received the gracious cooperation of the McLanes in the form of a signed quit-claim deed. It was a happy solution to a potentially "sticky wicket."

Not all right-of-way problems are this amicably solved. One sometimes confronts the type of person who will try to maximize a right-of-way situation and hold the solution hostage to virtual extortion. But certainly, Bill's clear thinking, a convivial approach to the sliver problem, coupled with the McLanes accommodating attitude, made the process enjoyable for all concerned.

A classical off-shoot of the right-of-way issue is the legal precept of "adverse possession." It's a most interesting legal principle which developed over the centuries in English Common Law. It protects those who may spend a lot of time and money developing and maintaining property through sincere belief that they own it, only to find that, technically, they don't have the proper title. Basically, it says that if an adjacent or encompassing property owner stands by and allows you to clean, gravel, and maintain a right-of-way over a period of years without calling into question your rights of ownership, then that person may actually have relinquished his rights in said property, and your efforts may have gained you ownership through "adverse possession."

One of the well known right-of-way situations exists, ironically, in the very center of Manhattan. When Rockefeller Center was constructed, a city street was created right in front of the R.C.A. building connecting 45th and 46th streets. It is actually a private roadway, but it is accessible to public vehicles 364 days a year. On the 365th day each year, however, the road is blocked off at each end and may not be accessed by traffic. In doing so, Rockefeller Center puts the world on notice that this is a private road and may not be claimed by the public nor the City by "adverse possession." Of course, now that the Japanese own Rockefeller Center I guess there's a private Japanese roadway right in the center of Manhattan. Peter Stuyvesant and Indian Chief Mahatahan, who sold him the island, must be turning over in their graves.

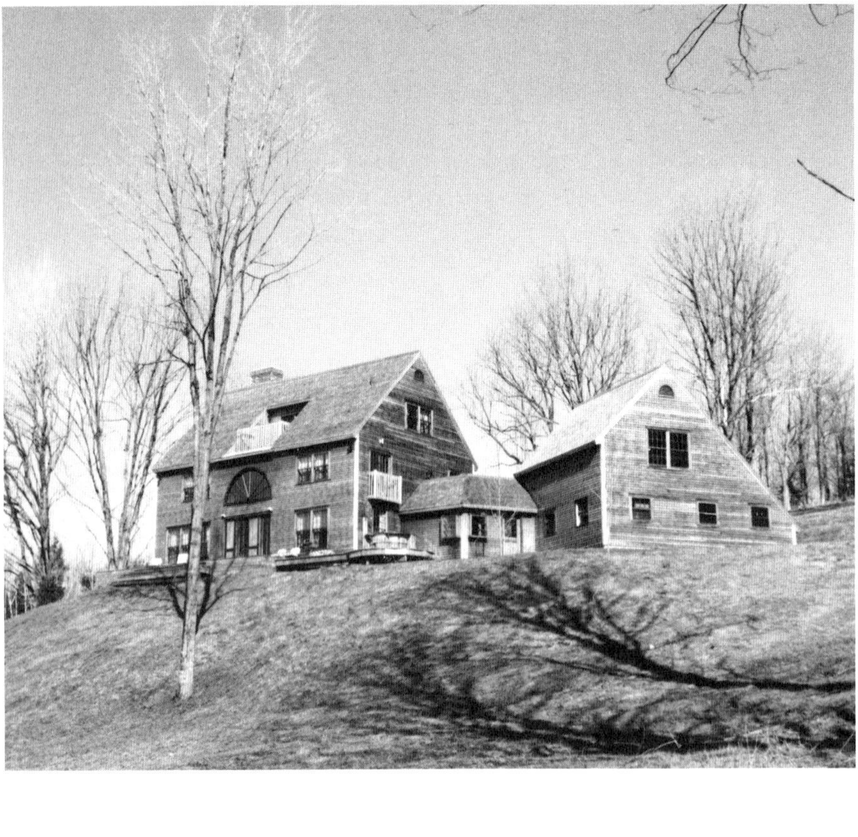

"Ineptitude"

Chapter 17

I'm always surprised by the preponderance of people who find it difficult to admit their frailties. It seems to me, for instance, if President Nixon had seen his way clear to own up to his indirect complicity in the Watergate break-in, that after a couple of days of heavy press coverage, the whole thing would have blown over, eclipsed by more pressing national issues. Yet many politicians and many business people are so afraid of admitting ignorance or error that they end up painting themselves into tight corners. Ironically, inasmuch as we are all flawed, imperfect human beings, we can much more easily relate to the weaknesses and imperfections of our fellow bumpkins than we can to the paragon in his ivory tower.

Back in my broadcast days in New York, I had a boss who called me in one day to cite my admission to a TV station owner that I had goofed in a particular respect. My boss flatly intoned, "Robert, we don't make mistakes here at the Katz Agency." From that time hence, with my TV firm I was condemned to waste a certain amount of time each day covering my errant tracks and anticipating challenges to my judgment.

But when I became my own boss in the real estate business, I early on, decided to dispense with the subterfuge. When I find my knowledge or my judgment wanting, my normal reply is, "I don't know the answer to that, but I'll find out," or "Sorry, I really am quite a slow learner, but I think we can rectify the situation," or "I do believe you're right; thanks for the input."

Of course, if I've made an error in judgment that has cost my client money or advantage, then I must take steps to compensate him, but generally, I've found that in facing issues and avoiding cover-ups, those issues usually become defused before they become costly. I guess I've been vindicated in this, because fortunately, I've never even been threatened with lawsuit.

Of course, in my case, the ability to admit error has been particularly helpful because over the years I've not always been "ept" . . . actually I've pulled some duzzies!

A couple of years ago, I escorted my esteemed client, Dr. Bruce Jorgensen of Philadelphia to a closing at the Vermont Federal Bank in Burlington. As we walked into the impressive foyer of the bank, we were greeted by an attractive receptionist who asked how she could help us.

"We have an appointment with Mr. Gaylord," I replied.

"Sir, I'm sorry, but we don't have a Mr. Gaylord," came her rejoinder.

"Please check again, young lady," I said, a little impatiently, "Mr. Gaylord is your executive vice president."

"INEPTITUDE"

My firm statement was followed by a pregnant pause, after which the young lady handed me a copy of the roster of the bank's executive staff . . . the letterhead read Vermont National Bank.

Beet red, I turned to my valued client and confessed, "One minor problem, Bruce. We seem to be in the wrong bank."

Now, fortunately, Bruce is possessed of a good sense of humor, so other than a few adroit barbs from my friendly client, no harm was done, and the thoroughly-vindicated young lady had the exquisite pleasure of directing us across the street and around the corner.

Kent and Natalie Mitchell were the victims of another comedy of errors, which, thanks to their understanding, ended short of debacle. After months of an exhaustive house search in which the price of fulfilling their requirements escalated from $150,000 to over twice that figure, the Mitchells had decided on a property which met several, but not all, of their criteria. They had decided to compromise their dreams through this acceptable structure, and they calculated that if they bought the property at under $300,000 and then invested another $40,000 in alterations and improvements, they would come close to what they wanted. We had arrived at a verbal agreement with the seller, and the only dangling participle was a meeting with the builder to review the proposed alterations and nail down the costs thereof.

I made an 8:30 a.m. appointment with the builder at the house in question, and arrived with the Mitchells at the appointed hour. By 9 a.m. the normally punctual builder had not arrived. By 9:30 a.m. the Mitchells were waxing understandably irritated.

"Are you sure you set this up, Bob?" they asked.

I assured them and called the builder's home, but got no answer, so Kent suggested we return to my office for possible messages. Still no word at the office, so my customers, with the patience of Job, suggested we take one last swing among the area's housing possibilities, and return later. (We found out the next day that the builder's mother had been rushed to the hospital that morning, and he had hastened to her side without thought of his appointment.)

So the morning shouldn't be a total loss, I took Natalie and Kent to the Retrovest House atop Brush Hill. It happens to be a magnificent 3-story, 4,400 square foot home with 15 acres and a breathtaking view, but I hadn't shown it to them previously because its $525,000 price tag was well out of their avowed range. We looked it over and they quickly confirmed that it was too much house for them in several respects, but as we left the driveway, Natalie asked about the lovely home on the adjoining ten acres above.

"It's also for sale," I replied, "but again, it's substantially out of your stated price range. There's another problem, the owners are absolutely insistent on an appointment with at least a day's notice."

"Well, I don't see any car there so let's take a look in the window," countered Natalie.

So with some trepidation, I drove up and we peered

"INEPTITUDE"

into the living room window. To our shock we found ourselves peering directly into the eyes of Mrs. Gruver, the owner. Midst my effusive apology, Mrs. Gruver finally volunteered, "Well, as long as you're here, you might as well come in and take a look." Incidentally, I always did love the house, but at the listed price, I still considered the episode an exercise in futility. Nonetheless, I dutifully followed along adding my enthusiastic confirmations here and there.

Then as we left I could see that a transformation had come over the Mitchells; they had just seen the house, that, in their mind's eye, they had been looking for all along. "What did you say the price of that house was?"

"A very firm $365,000" was my reply.

"Let's go back to the office and talk about it," said Kent.

By the time we got back to the office, Kent and Natalie's desire had crystallized. "We'll have to sell some things to swing it, but we want that house." So I got right on the phone with the listing broker and advised that we just might have a willing buyer.

Her first words were, "That's great, but I must tell you the Gruvers are unlikely to budge off that $465,000 price tag."

The Mitchells watched my jaw drop and the blood drain from my face. Kent claims I came close to fainting. I knew perfectly well that the price was $465,000; I had just offhandedly dropped a mere $100,000 in my quote. That may not be a big deal in Beverly Hills, but in Vermont that's virtually certifiable.

From 8:30 a.m. to that moment, the day had been a comedy of errors; I just wanted the earth to open and swallow me up . . . but then, with infinite patience, Kent said, "It did seem like a lot of house for the price . . . let's have a cup of coffee and explore ways to make it work."

To make a very long story short, we were able to sell the Mitchells' other property at an advantageous price; we successfully spun off some excess land from the Gruvers' ten acres; and despite my major gaffe, they hung in there and bought the house. But I do thank God I was working with kind, patient, and persevering people.

There have been other notable goofs along the way, like the day I showed Laura Riordan the Cummings [Jack] house on Spruce Peak. When my key easily entered the front door but wouldn't turn, I assumed it was a poor realtor's copy. Priding myself on my considerable skill as a second-story man, I adeptly gained entrance through the back porch . . . only to be subsequently confronted by the local constabulary with his gun akimbo. Turned out, unbeknownst to me, there were two Cummings houses on Spruce Peak, and I had just been guilty of "breaking and entering" into the wrong one. My customer was not impressed.

Another Keystone Comedy occurred when the Marshall House I had for sale had been taken off the market. I acknowledged the listing cancellation with the Marshalls, but subsequently, gave a moving company instructions on how to get to a house I had sold in the same general area. The mover confused my instructions,

"INEPTITUDE"

and pulled his furniture van into the Marshalls' drive. The mover had been told the key would be on the left hand side of the sill over the front door and, finding it there, felt sure he had the right house. He proceeded to unlock the door and unload the van. At that point, Mrs. Marshall returned home, confronted the scene and without a word to the mover, placed a panicked call to me.

"We distinctly told you we were taking the house off the market; we didn't want to sell . . . how could you have done this?"

"Emma, calm down. What are you talking about . . . I've done nothing!"

Eventually, cool heads prevailed and I instructed the mover to cease and desist and re-directed his operation. He was substantially off-base, but how could we have dreamed that both houses just happened to keep their "hidden" keys in exactly the same spot. I guess this sort of thing could happen more frequently in a homogeneous suburban setting like Levittown, but in Vermont, where houses are fewer and farther between, it was a bit of a shocking coincidence. It should also be a reminder that an experienced mover or realtor or burglar can often anticipate that "secret" hiding place for house keys.

At any rate, suffice it to say, in this, like many other businesses, it helps to be able to roll with the punches, and to be able to admit, "perfect, I ain't." Trying to maintain one's posture and balance while standing on a pedestal, can be very tedious and exhausting.

*"The Redcoats are Coming
. . . The Redcoats Are Coming"*

BRITTS
ANTIQUES
IMPORTERS
the Pub at Stone
the Fox & Hounds
FOOD
Inn
LODGING

"THE REDCOATS ARE COMING . . . THE REDCOATS ARE COMING"

CHAPTER 18

Northern Vermont, in this latter part of the 20th century, has experienced some recolonization by "The Mother Country." That is, we've been the happy migrant destination of a wide social strata of English expatriates. In Stowe alone, we now have "The English Pub," Ye Olde England Inn," "English Country Antiques," "Brit's Gift Shop" etc. Jack Lancaster, a British subject from Bermuda, now owns Stowe's largest estate.

Personally, I think the cross-pollination is terrific in that the British presence adds to the cosmopolitan flavor of the area. Thanks to the most challenging skiing in the East, Stowe has long entertained visitors from the Alpine countries of central Europe, and, being located next door to French Quebec, we enjoy increasing intercourse with the francophones. Now, the British are making their presence felt.

Pondering why this latter-day, British mini-invasion has taken place, a couple of factors come to mind: first, the unlimited social mobility of the U.S. and Vermont in particular. Although England's class system has moderated and economic opportunity has broadened, you still have to be born a gentleman, rarely can you achieve it. In England, your lineage, your school, and your accent still circumscribe your social stratum to a large extent.

I recently met a charming woman in England who has achieved a substantial degree of educational and commercial success, and has even developed a "cultured" accent in the process . . . but socially, sad to say, she now neither fits in with her old crowd nor the subtle snobbery of the upper class she now impinges upon. Professor Higgins worked a minor miracle on poor Eliza Doolittle, but in real life Eliza would have ended up neither fish nor foul in England, still "condemned by every word she uttered."

Such is definitely not the case in Vermont. You can be a prince or a pauper, speaking Boston Brahman, Brooklynese or Cockney, and you will be judged by whether you are an interesting person, and what kind of impact you make on the community . . . the social sky is the limit. A typical Stowe party will include a couple of captains of industry, coupon clippers, carpenters and grounds keepers. One well-known case involved wealthy scion Verner Z. Reed, III attending an upscale, black-tie party, and his return visit to the same premises at 8 a.m. the next morning in his role as garbage collector. In the old days, the guests at the posh Topnotch prized, above all else, an invitation to the ski bum's Bottom Notch where the real "in crowd" gathered.

Of course, we also enjoy in Vermont, a rolling countryside of mountains, hills and meadows like much of

England where their farmland has been preserved by strictly-zoned "green belts." Then, too, we do happen to speak the same language, (with notable exceptions), and when our English friends drive through the area, they go from Essex to Cambridge to Hyde Park to Hardwick which reads like the map of England.

I was the beneficiary of one particularly wonderful friendship thanks to this resettlement of Brits. George and Veronica Haywood moved to Stowe, to my very good fortune, possessed of the ultimate entrepreneurial spirit. George had reached the top executive echelon of Cadbury-Schweppes; he had also received the O.B.E. from Her Majesty in recognition of his intrepid services in Africa. But when he was passed over for the presidency of Schweppes, he decided it was time to fulfill a life-long dream and emigrate to the U.S. He did so via Canada and neighboring Montreal, so Stowe ended up being his U.S. destination.

George is one of those natural executives who is able to motivate a person to want to perform for him. I met him and Veronica at a neighbor's tea where he wasted no time in letting me know he liked what he'd heard about my real estate modus operandi. Without hesitation he gave me the assignment of finding them the ideal 10-acre parcel of land . . . land with seclusion, view and topography to accommodate a projected earth-sheltered home. He had the gift of investing confidence in me and making the whole project an exciting challenge. Of course I had a lot to learn about earth-sheltered homes, but situated properly in relation to the sun and views, they can open up to lovely vistas while still enjoying the advantages of natural insulation and privacy over much of the structure. With this requirement in mind, I found the ideal parcel of land; George and Veronica built the house and it ended up being a showplace and a wonderful setting for their frequent social and business events.

Over the next couple of years, I made other real estate investments for George and Veronica, and as our relationship developed they made me part of their stimulating social life. Having been stationed in Africa for a substantial part of their corporate lives, the Haywoods had learned to create their own entertainment. George, Veronica, their international friends, and their two charming British daughters really lit the place up for me.

After a couple of years, George said to me, "Bob, I've always wanted to own a large parcel of land. Now that you've shown me how to enhance and beautify a forest, I want to participate, hands-on. In England, 150 pristine acres would be prohibitively expensive, but in Vermont I could easily afford such a situation. Take your time, old boy, but when the right piece comes along I want you to buy it for me. I trust you; if you say it's the right property, we go." Once again, he had made the project an adventure . . . and once again, I'd have thrown myself in front of a moving car for George Haywood.

Nothing shook loose for a few months, and then one day I dropped into McCarthy's Restaurant to find my friend, Andy Gergely, with a large land map spread over the counter, making a strong pitch to Marvin Gameroff as a prospective buyer. As I passed by, Andy said to

Marvin, "Now, here's a guy who could find me a buyer for the land." I stopped, studied the map, and recognized it as a large parcel in Sterling Valley which I'd long known and valued. It turned out the parcel had come into the hands of a Providence bank through an estate settlement, and they'd put it on the market.

In response to Andy's off-hand remark, I nonchalantly enjoined, "If you'll co-broke on your listing, I think I can sell the 144 acres in about an hour." He and Marvin both chuckled at my little joke . . . but I knew it wasn't a joke.

I left the restaurant and headed straight for Haywood's office. Unfortunately George was in Kansas City, and Veronica was deep in conference with a couple of attorneys. Therefore, I just left the map with a note in longhand extolling the property as the piece we'd been looking for.

I returned in an hour, and found Veronica still deep in conference . . . but this time she signaled to me in sign language and formed the silent words, "We'll take it; draw up the contract."

I replied in gesticular lip-sync, "You can't buy it 'til George comes back and we walk it together."

Again, over the impatient voices of her conferees, she mouthed, "We want it NOW!"

So I succumbed, got a $5,000 deposit check from her secretary, drew up the agreement and was back to Gergely's office within two hours of the original encounter. I walked in, apologized for being an hour late, dropped the check and contract on Andy's desk, and simply said, "Sold!" Andy was flabbergasted; grumbled something like he could have sold the property himself in a couple more days.

"Andy, don't look a gift horse in the mouth. We both just made $5,000 in an afternoon! Smile, already!"

When George returned from Kansas City, he, Veronica and I put on our hiking boots and walked the land. Fortunately they loved it, as they had committed to it long before they ever saw it.

Eventually, a great opportunity opened for the Haywoods on the West Coast. They have become a major factor in the warehousing business from Washington to California with their own fishing fleet to boot. I couldn't be happier about their success, but I sure do miss them. Stowe lost some of its flair and pizzazz when these English cousins of ours departed.

I did have one wonderful reprise. Just before the Haywoods moved West, and after I'd resold their property at a substantial profit, they scheduled a trip to London for a series of parties celebrating their silver wedding anniversary.

George said, "Robert, old chap, why don't you invest one of those commission checks in a ticket to London and join our merry throng."

"Done, George. I wouldn't miss it for the world."

So I made my first trip to England in fifteen years; partook of the movable feast celebrating their marriage with Brits from every corner of the Empire; reconnected with my British genes; and even better, reconnected with a charming English lady I had met at Cambridge University fifteen years previously.

As I've said, the Haywoods lit up my life. They're the kind of clients/friends I wish for all my fellow realtors . . . but be sure, when the Haywoods of this world come your way, to respond with the same generosity, effort and love they offer to you.

ARAGON
End of the original dynasty

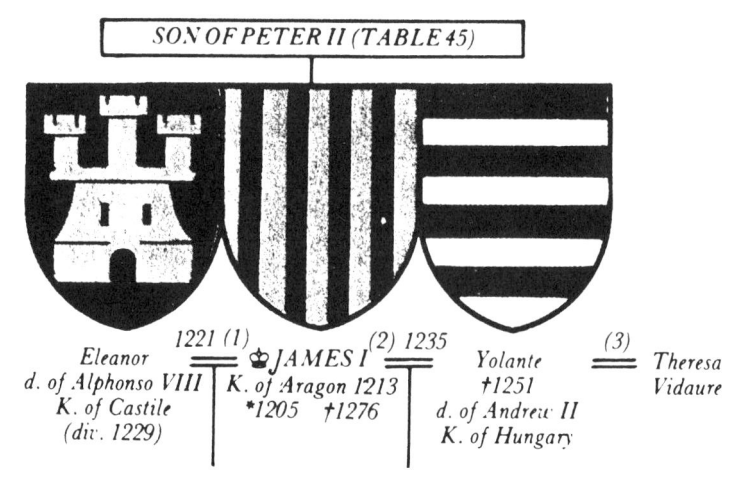

SON OF PETER II (TABLE 45)

	1221 (1)		(2) 1235		(3)	
Eleanor	=	♛*JAMES I*	=	*Yolante*	=	*Theresa*
d. of Alphonso VIII		*K. of Aragon 1213*		†*1251*		*Vidaure*
K. of Castile		**1205 †1276*		*d. of Andrew II*		
(div. 1229)				*K. of Hungary*		

"The Duke of Aragon"

CHAPTER 19

"THE DUKE OF ARAGON"

Dealing in real estate in a recreational area offers great variety and fascinating projects, but there is a downside . . . we seem to attract many of the oddballs and phonies that are inexorably drawn to resort areas. I guess the most colorful character to confound my life in recent years was the "Duke of Aragon."

The Duke walked into my office one hot day in August and promptly announced that he wanted to acquire the "most prestigious property in the area." There was question in my mind from the outset about the "Duke's" authenticity, but when a man is talking over a half million dollars, it's hard not to give him the benefit of the doubt.

Of course, he explained that most of his money was residing in Swiss, Italian, and Spanish banks, so confirming his financial capability would have been difficult at best. The man definitely had the panache to go with the title; spoke all the romance languages fluently; and seemed to know where all the social "bodies were buried" from Newport to Palm Beach to Biarritz. He had already rented a Stowe house which he had punctuated with a few Louis XIV pieces under an impressive family coat of arms. He claimed to be presently married to an Italian princess from whom he was estranged, and I later even heard a rumor from Montreal sources that one of his wives had died under very questionable circumstances.

At any rate, he did seem serious about wanting to buy a major property, and he deftly stroked my ego by repeating that I was considered "The Oracle of Delphi" in high-end real estate. Complications arose immediately, however, when I became convinced, by the drift of his conversation, that his romantic preference was the male gender, and that his day began, sustained itself and ended with "spirits fermenti." One of his endearing practices was to call me at 6:30 each morning; make sure I was thoroughly awakened and thoroughly agitated; and then I assume, go back to bed for his "noblesse oblige" mid-morning siesta. Despite his obvious shortcomings, he was also an unabashed snob; one of his favorite bon mots being "chaque un a son mauvais gout." Part of his consummate alcoholic denial was to consistently look down his nose at the common folk.

Looking back, I realize that what the Duke craved even more than alcohol was attention. Trading on his avowed intention to make a "major" real estate commitment, he managed to drag me around to view half the houses in the Stowe area that summer while I tended to his many idiosyncrasies.

Now, Stowe does happen to have one real mansion in the traditional sense. The Old Lambert Place on Tabor Hill is truly built on the grand scale. My farmhouse, roof and all, would fit nicely in the cathedral-ceilinged living room. Its history is almost a duplicate of "The Unsinkable Molly Brown" story. Back in the '30s, John Lambert of Lambert Pharmaceutical (Listerine, Ipana, etc.) had come skiing in Stowe from St. Louis, had broken his leg, and was nurtured back to health by a nurse from the Morrisville area.

Impacted by her tender loving care, he fell in love with this unpretentious local Vermont girl, married her, and took her back to introduce her to St. Louis society. The poor young lady found herself out of her depth in high society, so Lambert brought her back to Vermont and ensconced her in the Lambert mansion in Stowe, a palatial home replete with servants' quarters, etc. In spite of this effort, the marriage eventually foundered, and the Lambert Mansion has really not been lived in for almost 50 years.*

In examining the house, I found sheet music on the baby grand piano dating back to the '30s that had not been disturbed since that time. I found a crossword puzzle on the end table, half-completed, that was dated July 1938. The place is a true anachronism, evoking a strong aura of a bygone time of wealth and privilege.

As I might have guessed, it was the Lambert House that the Duke zeroed in on. With his assurance that he

---

*Since this chapter was first penned a year ago, a tasteful, affluent branch of the Bacardi family has purchased and restored the mansion.

was prepared to purchase the property, I proceeded with an elaborate inspection of the premises, which had not enjoyed progressive maintenance in many years. The place turned out to be in remarkably good shape with the exception of the huge carrying beams in the basement. The house was so massive that its weight had compromised the integrity of those beams, but we came up with a solution involving the insertion of steel I-beams, etc. As the Duke was "awaiting a large cash transfer from Switzerland," I naturally paid for the inspection and the engineers plans for structural augmentation.

We finally arranged for a meeting with the syndicate that currently held title to the Lambert Place. The four gentlemen that made up the syndicate flew up from Massachusetts on the assurance that we had a serious buyer in tow. I briefed the Duke on the asking price, the possible area of negotiation, the contingencies upon which he should insist, and the background of the sellers. We went into the meeting, optimistically assured by the Duke that he would bring along a $20,000 escrow deposit check that would satisfy these gentlemen of his serious intentions.

As you may have guessed, the meeting was a farce and a disaster. The Duke called upon every obfuscating, stalling tactic imaginable. The meeting ended in anger and frustration by the owners, and I came to the stark realization that I had just wasted half of my summer playing wet nurse to a master of manipulation who had neither the intention nor capability to buy anything of substance. Of course, the Duke claimed that the negotiations had broke down because of my ineptitude and the intransigence of the sellers, but in reality, I had just been the producer of his latest dramatic production, and aided him in gaining some of the attention he so eagerly sought.

The only redeeming feature of the whole, costly, embarrassing episode was the final crystallization of my resolve that I would no longer deal with the Duke even if he was truly planning to buy the whole town of Stowe, lock, stock, and barrel . . . life is just too short! It also led me to decide that hence I would sell only properties for reasonable people to reasonable customers; that I would no longer make dollars the determinant of my choices of involvement, and would leave the arrogant, or manipulative types to stronger or more patient members of the real estate community. Surprisingly, in the ten years since that decision, it has cost me very little money and helped preserve a large part of my sanity.

About six months after the Duke left town under somewhat of a cloud, I got one of my old 6:30 a.m. calls. It was "Himself" calling from Palm Beach to advise me that he had "just purchased a major property on the oceanfront" and would have spent the money in Stowe instead had I been a little more cooperative and helpful. Now I was taught to be polite to my fellow man, but this time I burst out laughing in the Duke's face. He just had to make one last effort to hit me where he thought it would hurt. Punishment, I guess, for withdrawing my undivided attention from his various machinations.

Having, fortunately, put that episode behind me, my only lingering question about people of that ilk, is how much of their fantasies they actually believe at the time they are weaving the tapestries of their imaginations. I think, to a greater or lesser degree, they are self-hypnotized into believing the persona and the figments they create.

Self-delusion can be a powerful thing, and of course, we brokers can be contributory to that delusion, like the mark who buys the "stolen" diamond ring from the confidence man at a fraction of its "real value." We so want that bogus buyer to be real, that we let the lure of the big commission suck us in when our better judgment should see the handwriting on the wall.

I wonder where and on what gullible broker the Duke is playing his games these days.

"Selling the Sizzle"

Chapter 20

Jack Latimore was one of those eternal bachelors for whom the chase is generally more exciting than the conquest. He could have been dubbed a "womanizer" except that he was much too forthright and considerate for that indictment. Besides, he usually stopped short of compromising the virtue of any lady who didn't want to be compromised. Nonetheless, the hunt for the fair sex was his all-consuming preoccupation.

Jack was a frequent guest at the Topnotch, but one day he decided it was time to acquire his own vacation home in the ski country, and he gave me the assignment. We'd been looking at homes in a somewhat desultory way, but Jack said, "I'll know it when I see it," and we hadn't seen it. We were sharing Sunday night dinner at the Topnotch with some friends, when Walter Aigner happened in and we invited him to join us. I had the presence of mind to recall that Walter, a builder, was just completing an attractive 3-bedroom "spec" house in Mansfield View.

Walter's area of creativity was stone masonry. He was wont to create a spectacular bathroom and build the house around the bathroom. In the current case, he had found a site with an exquisite woodland spring bubbling up through the natural rock formation. Augmenting this natural setting with masonry and inlaid tile, Walter had created a "Roman" bath that would have been the envy of Caesar and his court. The house itself was actually designed around this masonry masterpiece, and the fortunate happenstance that Walter had joined our dinner group jogged my instinct that a mention of this sensual bath would whet Jack Latimore's appetite.

Waiting until dessert, I turned to Walter and said, "that's a very attractive vacation home you're building in Mansfield View, but I think you've gone overboard with that prurient, immoral bathroom. It's downright pagan!"

Latimore immediately turned to me and said, "What pagan bathroom? Why haven't you shown this place to me!"

"Jack," I said, "I've always considered you at least fair in your dealing with young women; this would be giving you a leg up (you'll pardon the expression) you don't deserve or need."

"Whose side are you on anyway!" he growled. "You're my real estate agent and I want to see that house tomorrow."

Of course, the unfair advantage was mine. Once having seen the "pagan" bathroom, Jack just had to have the place and it was one of the easiest sales I've ever made. The sizzle had definitely sold the steak.

To give credit where credit is due, Walter was really ahead of his time. In affluent yuppiedum today, everyone seems to be going for the jacuzzi, the whirlpool bath, and other sophisticated gimmicks known to realtors as "bells and whistles." It's somewhat akin to the options on the modern sporty cars and has contributed to the escalating prices on much real estate . . . but I've yet to see a bathroom approach the seductive ambiance of the one that Jack Latimore bought.

Aqua Pura

*"As Long as Grass Shall Grow
or Waters Flow"*

Courtesy of Vt. Dept. of Travel and Tourisr

Chapter 21

When King George of England bequeathed large tracts of land in Vermont to various of his designated settlers, he set aside in each town or district, certain parcels of 100 acres or so for the support of religious, medical or educational institutions. These were designated as "lease lots" or "glebe lots." In effect they would be amongst lands privately owned, but were not taxable by the respective towns or municipalities. Instead, the owner or "leaseholder" was obliged to pay a leasehold rent each year to the designated public institution, i.e., the benefit of the local minister or local school or "The Society for the Propagation of the Gospel in Foreign Parts."

When I started selling Vermont land in 1962, some parcels were paying yearly fees to the University of Vermont, some to the Vermont Medical Center, and some to the Episcopal Archdiocese of Vermont (former Church of England). Although these designees had been updated over the years, the amount of the lease rent had not, so there were parcels of 100 acres which paid only $7.50 yearly to the designated institution in lieu of taxes. The

AQUA PURA

adjacent 100 acres of so-called private land might be paying up to $1,000.00 in town property taxes, so "lease land" was a terrific bargain while it lasted.

The only complication was that a buyer of such a parcel of "lease land" did not receive the normal deed. Instead, he received a leasehold or perpetual lease on said land "for as long as grass shall grow or waters flow." (This was eventually evidenced by a quit claim deed but not a warranty deed.) Unless Vermont was to evolve into a Sahara Desert, that was about as permanent a designation as one could wish. Nonetheless, I did lose a major sale because the prospective buyer, a rigid Philadelphia lawyer, adamantly insisted, "I don't want to lease the land. I want to buy it." All my reassurances to the contrary, he walked away from a great land buy, (i.e. 100 acres for $11,000) ostensibly because this old Vermont law wasn't covered in his law books. He was an inflexible gent and I simply couldn't get him to understand that, in Vermont, grass was going to grow and water was going to flow in perpetuity.

The "lease land law" was finally repealed and superseded back in the late '60s, and fee-simple deeds were exchanged for the leases, so that nowadays everyone is paying their fair share of taxes to the towns, but it was a fascinating anachronism while it lasted.

"Water Doesn't Flow Upstream"

Talking about the flow of water reminds me of a problem I took to a Vermont lawyer regarding a very complicated requirement by an environmental permit on a building site. The septic permit document, dealing with waste disposal on this lot, was a nightmare. A particular state bureaucrat with a technical bent had spelled out maintenance requirements on this simple septic system which would call for prohibitive expenditures in time and money down the years. The attorney I consulted couldn't legally advise me in contradiction with state authority nor contravene the specifications in the permit . . . he simply said, "water doesn't flow upstream." In that one simple phrase, he was saying, "install the septic system responsibly, maintain the system reasonably, and don't worry about Big Brother 'cause he hasn't the time or tenacity to look over your shoulder down the years."

For we real estate agents that phrase "water doesn't flow upstream" also has a pejorative connotation. Human nature is such that when a client wants something badly, he'll do anything or promise anything within reason to effect that acquisition. Once we've accomplished what he wants, he may be less likely to remember and reward us for our work in helping him get there. One of the biblical parables was of the six lepers who sought the Messiah's touch and were miraculously healed. They all went away dancing and jumping for joy . . . but only one of the six remembered to come back and thank Him.

You may also remember the beautiful old English ballad of the "Golden Vanity" wherein the ship was bottled up, outgunned, and doomed by the Spanish Galleon. The captain of the Golden Vanity gathered the crew and offered to grant any wish of that brave seaman who would swim out to the galleon that night and plant an explosive charge on her hull. One seaman volunteered and swam successfully to scuttle the Spanish galleon. He returned to the cheers of his crew mates and was honored by the captain, who commanded, "now state any wish." The seaman declared, "I claim the hand of the captain's beautiful daughter in marriage" . . . The captain's memory suddenly became very selective and the common seaman's tragic reward was to be keel-hauled and drowned in "the cold North Sea" for his presumptuousness. The battle crisis had been solved, and the brave sailor had become expendable. C'est la vie!

In less dramatic forms, there are many instances in real estate when buyers or sellers will promise most any reward to the agent who will effectively solve their pressing problem. The good intention is there at the moment, but for the subsequent peace of mind of all concerned, and a fair recompense for your efforts, you'd better have it in writing. Robert Frost said, "good fences make good neighbors," and in real estate the written agreement is "the good fence" that reminds all concerned of their prior commitment.

Wetlands

One of the main environmental thrusts at present is the preservation of wetlands. I always thought wetlands were just a swampy, mosquito breeding blight, but I've learned that wetlands are a necessary part of our ecosystem, supplying habitat for migratory bird life, replenishing essential water aquifers, and sustaining the chain of the natural life cycle. Where major swamp or coastal areas are filled in or drained to create building sites, as in many sections of Florida or along Chesapeake Bay, man's tinkering with nature can potentially upset the ecosystem. In Vermont, for example, efforts to drain the historic and pervasive Victory Bog were a legitimate concern of the environmental lobby, and were blocked by legislation.

However, in my opinion, "wetlands" are now being used as a general weapon to frustrate as much development as possible in Vermont and in many cases the legitimate purposes of the legislation are being manipulated by radical environmentalists.

For instance, in Stowe there is a, now, seasonally-wet area directly east of the village. This tract of land used to be part of a going farm evidenced by historic photographs of the rolling meadows that covered the area. But over the years beavers have bottled up the drainage through this section and today approximately 19 acres of the total 94 acres of this property has been designated "wetlands."

As this general area east of town is the only logical and viable location for a much-needed extension of the Village, hundreds of thousands of dollars have been invested in a legitimate, low-density plan to extend the Village into this area with a mix of stores, and affordable housing in harmony with the historical and traditional Village motif.

Aqua Pura

The proposal is to channel the swampy sections into linked ponds, keep a majority of the 94 acres in a natural state, and proceed with a balanced development of the area. But now that 19 acres of this strategic location has been designated "wetlands," any plan to gather or drain the water and bring this tract back to its old historical condition has been estopped and the State Environmental Department, the U.S. Corps of Engineers, and various environmental groups have descended on the Town, virtually killing the project.

The rationale is to perpetuate the habitat of a handful of hardy beavers, muskrats, and birds. Were this a rare, endangered aquatic ecosystem, its preservation would be justified, but northern Vermont enjoys hundreds of thousands of undeveloped acres offering a plethora of alternative areas for migratory birds, etc. which don't happen to be in a critical Village location.

This situation is illustrative of the need to weigh competing priorities, and to try to establish a sense of proportion between the legitimate aims of preserving the environment, meeting human and public needs, and rewarding major monetary investment in responsible growth.

The Eager Beaver and Herbiveral Eminent Domain

I don't mean to demean the beaver. Surely the beaver is one of the most fascinating animals in North America. He's very aptly dubbed "eager," because he's a relentless and indefatigable worker. One of the major beaver dam complexes in northern Vermont covers 60 acres of former rich, farm bottomland next to my property on Gregg Hill in Waterbury. The beavers have appropriated this once-agriculturally-productive farmland by gnawing down most of the area's foliage and building a series of dams and ponds. I've learned a lot about these fascinating creatures by just observing their activities over the years; activities that are ingeniously interrelated.

When the beavers decide on a new habitat, they start by felling a wide swath of trees and bushes next to a stream. Then they painstakingly weave a dam across the path of said stream, constructed of branches and twigs packed together with mud by use of their powerful, flat, leathery tails. By instinct, they leave this mesh just porous enough that the stream can continue to trickle through without blowing out the dam. But as soon as possible, other members of the clan get to work on satellite dams downstream, so that eventually there will be a series of dams and ponds leading to one another. It took me a while before I recognized the method in their madness. Eventually I realized that the dams, in sequence, protect the colony from the sporadic torrential downpour that would swell the stream and blow out any impediment in its path; i.e., the series of dams slow down the flow, so that the main dam is spared the impact of a major deluge.

The beaver's unique dwelling is the "hogan" or house built in the middle of the pond which can only be accessed from underwater, and is thus impregnable to its natural, non-aquatic enemies. As they are workers, not

AQUA PURA

fighters, their other defense is their early-warning system which is a mighty slap on the water's surface by their wide, flat tails. At times when I've forgotten about this phenomenon, and jogged past the beaver pond at night, I've been virtually lifted out of my running shoes by a slap tantamount to a gunshot. I've also watched with a chuckle when my golden retriever has swum out after the beavers only to have these aquatic animals toy with his efforts and slap tails all around him. The retriever is no match on their "playing field."

We had a unique example of the tenacity of the beavers on Gregg Hill a couple of years ago. As the beavers were busily decimating the flora and extending their series of dams along the stream, they came to the culvert under the town road. Treating this as any other dam site, they proceeded, each night, to fill and pack the culvert with branches and twigs, so that the road was swamped and in jeopardy of being washed out. The town maintenance men would have to arrive each day and laboriously yank all the woven material out of the culvert. This time-and-labor consuming battle went on for many weeks, and as it wasn't beaver-trapping season, the Town couldn't do away with the frustrating critters nor blow out their main dams because of environmental regulations. Finally someone came up with the idea of a large steel grate that was welded together and fitted over the end of the culvert. It was constructed so that is could be raised, cleaned and re-lowered; a fortunate foresight, for ever since, the beavers continue to weave this grid with branches and twigs nightly. For now, the roadbed has been saved, but there is no clear winner in this conflict between man and beast.

And now, thanks to the federal and state wetlands legislation, the beavers can have an even more telling impact on private landowners. As the state environmental law is now being interpreted, once a beaver colony has flooded an area, it automatically comes under the definition of "wetland," and may not be drained or retrieved for farming or development without very special dispensation. This means that if a person owns a large tract of land at arm's length on which he may have been paying taxes for many years with the idea of eventually building on or subdividing the property . . . and if, in the owner's absence, the beavers have dammed up the stream coursing through that land, then the beavers and the State, by what I call "herbivorous eminent domain," have effectively taken over control of that area and, by law, the owner cannot put that land back in its original, natural state. As there is a very limited beaver-trapping season in Vermont, the tax-paying landowner may be waging another losing battle in competition with the eager environmentalist and the eager beaver.

Let me mount my soapbox for a moment because again I think we need to weigh conflicting priorities and apply some sense of proportion in these matters. Private ownership of property is a keystone of the free-enterprise system. We need to strike a balance between the perpetuation of our ecosystems, and the rights of the tax-paying landowner, whose taxes and creative efforts ultimately pay for that perpetuation. We've recently, and belatedly, become aware that the Eastern Bloc communist countries, where private ownership of real estate was denied, had consistently wreaked much greater harm to their environment than had the democratic West.

So let's maintain some balance and not too hastily dissipate our country's cherished rights of private ownership . . . because in Vermont, at least, even among development-oriented property owners, there is generally a sense of proportion and responsibility to the land that will always keep "the grass growing and the waters flowing."

"Hanging In There"

"It Ain't Over 'Til the Fat Lady Sings"

Sepp Ruschp?

Courtesy of Stowe Reporte

Chapter 22

I've found, over the years, that the sequence in a major real estate deal goes something like this: it starts out looking like a "piece of cake or a ripe plum about to fall off the tree"; then it starts to get complicated; then it looks impossible to mediate and begins to appear dead in the water; and then, if the gods smile, it becomes miraculously resuscitated and actually comes to a close. It usually takes patience, faith, and perseverance to hang in there and make it happen. "Faint heart never won fair maiden," nor a major real estate deal.

Early on, I was plying my modest real estate trade in Stowe when I got a call from Bruce Nourjian, one of the ski instructors from the Mt. Mansfield Company, the parent organization that controls all the skiing operations and a great deal more in this resort area. He called to say he was giving private lessons to a "high roller" who was interested in buying a major tract of land as near as possible to the ski slopes. Such a request definitely gets one's attention, so I set about researching every possibility. As much of the land surrounding the

Stowe/Mansfield Ski Area is state forest and Mt. Mansfield itself owns the bulk of the remainder, those possibilities are very limited. The logical situation turned out to be the approximate 450 acres up near the ski areas owned by the Adams Mill Corp. of Moscow, VT. They had used this natural wooded area over the years as an ongoing, managed source of timber for their woods product plant in the Moscow section of Stowe. The Adams Mill is the oldest operating business in the area, dating back to the 1700s, and is a completely family-owned and operated enterprise. So when I approached them about selling this tract there was much intra-family debate and consultation. After months of visits and negotiations wherein I talked volumes and the laconic members of the Adams family offered a paucity of response, we finally arrived at a tentative agreement of sale, and the proposal was submitted to the family attorney. To my great disappointment, I was subsequently advised that due to tax implications of a "Chapter S" Corporation, they were precluded from selling the land.

Had they vetted this possible sale with their attorney at the outset, they could have saved me six months of work: such are the vagaries of the real estate business. But in my efforts in the meanwhile, I had taken the initiative to approach Mr. Sepp Ruschp, the prestigious director of the Mt. Mansfield Company to see if his company would consider granting to my potential buyer, a right-of-way access through Mansfield Company property that would greatly simplify access to the Adams' 450 acres. Mr. Ruschp, who was a very decent and honorable Austrian gentleman, surprised me by readily agreeing to grant the approximate 800 ft. key right-of-way. So when our deal with the Adams family fell through, I remembered his graciousness, and drove up to his office at the Mountain to advise him of the demise of the deal, but also to reiterate my appreciation of his gracious offer.

I had almost reached the door in leaving Mr. Ruschp's office when he very evenly stated, "You never know, perhaps ve might sell your customer some of our own landt." Well now, no one in these parts ever dreamed that the Mt. Mansfield Company, (which was then part of the C.V. Starr Insurance Co., which in turn is part of A.I.G., one of the nation's largest corporations) would sell any of its land. Fortunately for my puposes, however, they were at that very moment considering a condominium development near the Mountain that would require considerable additional capital investment. So I froze in my tracks, turned back to Mr. Ruschp and was suddenly back in negotiation for my customer.

It turned out that what Mr. Ruschp was tentatively offering was 200 acres of strategically located land, and after we negotiated all the attendant costs in complicated road construction, and power installation into this mountainous area, etc., we agreed on a do-able price for the 200 acres and arrived at verbal agreement with my N.Y. customer . . . effectively opening up Phase 2 of my odyssey.

Of course the Mt. Mansfield Company insisted on a long laundry list of protective covenants, i.e. limited timber removal, 5-acre average density per subdivided parcel, architectural oversight, etc., but all of these restrictions actually made sense for both parties in preserving the value of the property for all concerned, so again, verbal agreement was reached and the buyer signed the contract.

Now came time for presentation of the contract to the Mt. Mansfield/C.V. Starr Corporation. The ironic thing was that because the corporation didn't want to commit itself in any way until they had completely vetted the potential buyer and his reputation, the only written information of any kind on the deal had come from my end, i.e. from my ancient manual typewriter. So when it came time for me to fly to N.Y. to meet the president of C.V. Starr Corporation via the company jet, the document in my hot little hand was a contract typed on my ancient Royal manual. It was a complicated eight-page agreement covering every exigency I could think of, but I was still going to meet with the president, comptroller, and legal counsel of C.V. Starr Corporation midst the concrete canyons of Wall Street, equipped with a pretty amateurish document.

As Mr. Ruschp and I were ushered into the exquisite board room replete with white-coated waiters to serve our coffee, I suddenly felt very inadequate, strongly questioning my presumption at being there. As Robert Benchley had written about his visit to the dentist, I suddenly wished that the building would collapse and I'd be swallowed up and not have to face this formidable phalanx of superior financial minds. But, notwithstanding my terror, the contract was finally placed on the inlaid board room table. Mr. Tweedy, the president, read it without smile or comment and passed it to his accountant, who read it without smile or comment and passed it to the attorney. After what seemed an interminable pause Mr. Tweedy said, "Well, I think it's a reasonable deal; what do you think, Frank?" . . .

"I think with some minor modifications, it will work" . . . "What do you think George?"

"I think it does what we want it to do, Gordon" . . . whence Mr. Tweedy turned to me and said, "Mr. Murray, it looks like you have a deal."

As Eddie Condon remarked when he first heard young Bix Beiderbeck blow his trumpet, "It came out like a woman saying, 'yes!'" . . . instead of being exposed as a presumptuous fraud, I'd been treated with respect and had pulled off a major coup; I felt like I'd died and gone to heaven.

But in real estate, it's never over 'til the fat lady sings and the deed is passed, so we set a closing on the property for 30 days hence. That time was well spent working out details, covenant refinements, and bank financing for my buyer's operating funds. We were set for a May 28th closing. A week prior I called my buyer at his New York office to review details and was advised that he was out of town. Repeated calls that week got the same answer without any forwarding phone number. By May 26th I was panicked, and finally on May 27th my buyer returned my call. It was a shocker!

He had just experienced his first set-back in a meteoric rise in the construction field. A major bank had withdrawn its commitment on a sizable loan and, with abject apology, he said he would have to renege on his commitment and just hoped we could salvage a major portion of his deposit.

Now, having had my seller pull the rug out in the first phase of this operation, I was hit with a last minute cancellation by my buyer in Phase 2.

With effusive apology, I had to call Mt. Mansfield Company and the C.V. Starr Corporation and felt extreme embarrassment at having "diddled" these busy gentlemen. Ironically, the one who took the news hardest of all was Bruce, the ski instructor, who had produced the prospective buyer in the first place. Seems he had been promised a major role in the development operation by the New York buyer and now his bubble, too, had burst. It also happened that he was scheduled to crew on a yacht in Narragansett Bay that weekend, so I solaced him that he could at least get far away from the situation and forget all about the mountains.

Then the miracle happened. The yacht owner commented on Bruce's depression and ineptitude in that weekend's race, and Bruce, in response, explained his tale of woe about the lost real estate deal. "Don't worry about it!" was the affluent yachtsman's reply. "Sounds like the very type of project I'd like to undertake at this stage of my life, and you guys have done all the groundwork; I'll take over the deal!"

I could hardly believe my ears when Bruce came back Monday; the twice moribund deal was alive again, and this time the buyer didn't even need a bank commitment. Of course we still had to convince the C.V. Starr

Corporation that this new buyer was capable and tasteful and of sound reputation, etc., but after another trip to the N.Y. board room, he passed muster and we finally closed . . . we closed . . . WE CLOSED!!

The course of true love and real estate transactions rarely run smoothly but if you "accentuate the positive," "keep your hand on the plow," and hang in there, they may actually happen.

Punch

"The High Wire Act"

Chapter 23

One of the main precepts of small business venture is "never go into an investment undercapitalized." It's great to have the intestinal fortitude and initiative to risk one's fortunes in a new and exciting enterprise, but it's also prudent to have an extra cushion against a hard landing or a rainy day. In ski country where snow is the "sine qua non," that can be a literal rainy day.

George and Estelle Smith had had it up to here with urban Long Island. The quality of life in that megalopolis that now extends, virtually unbroken, from Boston to Baltimore, has largely deteriorated except for those fortunate few who can insulate themselves deep in suburbia. In the face of the school and drug crisis, etc., Vermont can look awfully attractive to a family with school-age children. George and Estelle made their position crystal clear to me. "We need a small business with a built-in living situation, where we can generate enough income to make the mortgage payments and keep food on the table."

There's nothing that sounds better to a realtor than a modest, obtainable goal. I happened to have just the small motel listed to meet all their criteria: i.e., 10 units on four acres fronting on one of Stowe's main arteries. This in combination with a snug, three-bedroom owner's apartment, and a small remodelable in-house restaurant facility . . . all at the bargain-basement price of $160,000. Of course, the current owners had run the business into the ground; he was involved in an off-premises printing business and she basically didn't like people. It is amazing how many people get into the hostelry business who really don't like dealing with the public. In some cases, I think they buy an inn or lodge as a solution to their anti-social proclivities. Invariably, it just compounds the problem.

At any rate, we had the ideal "willing buyer/willing seller" situation and in short order, we had a signed agreement of sale. As so typically is the case in real estate, at that point the work really started. George and Estelle's prerequisite house sale on Long Island was repeatedly delayed, and when their financial statement arrived for the bank's scrutiny, it fell short of the asset and income requirements needed. Nonetheless, I hung in there and after an exhaustive canvas of almost every bank in northern Vermont, I finally approached the U.S. Small Business Administration in Montpelier. I had been warned that the red tape at the S.B.A. was virtually prohibitive, but I was happily surprised to find that they really were receptive to helping this small business gain a foothold. So after a reasonable number of forms in quadruplicate, we finally secured the loan guarantee needed by my customers. Of course, they were still in Long

Island, so I did all their paper work and mortgage negotiations for them. I don't think they fully grasped the gymnastics I performed to procure that mortgage, and maybe I insulated them from the realities of U.S. S.B.A mortgage finance in the process.

In due time, they took possession of the motel, and fortunately, Estelle did like people. She had a wonderful caring, nurturing quality that made her guests feel at home. Although the place was hardly the Taj Mahal (in Agra nor Atlantic City), she made people feel loved and wanted, so the business grew. George was mechanically handy, and a great raconteur, so he added to the working order and the ambiance of the place.

Then after a couple of years of operation, the equation changed . . . George having become somewhat unfulfilled with his handyman role, was offered a lucrative position with a builder in the Boston area, so with the motel pretty well organized, he became a bi-weekly commuter from the Boston area. Estelle continued to run the guest operation including sporadic busloads who required meals on the weekends.

Now, we all tend to apply ourselves to that phase of our business that comes most naturally and which we most enjoy. Estelle greeted and counseled, and cooked and made people feel wanted . . . but she paid much less attention to the fiscal, accounting or progressive maintenance ends of the business. There was, perhaps, also a sense of isolation and loneliness with George away for long periods. However, the business still appeared to be in a healthy state.

Finally, at the end of about 4 years with George pulling down a substantial income, they decided to sell the motel and build themselves their dream home. It was late November of that year and Estelle was looking forward to a lucrative ski season, so she said she'd consider signing a contract for sale but wouldn't pass deed or give occupancy until March 15th of the following year.

With that limitation, I began trying to find a buyer at a price about twice the amount they'd paid for the property. In very short order, a retiring couple came along willing to pay almost the full asking price . . . the hooker being that they insisted on occupancy within 30 days . . . by Christmas. On that point, Estelle wouldn't budge. She had all her beloved clientele scheduled for Christmas and the ski season, and she wouldn't depart until March 15th. I admonished her that the "time to hunt bear is when they're out and about," but to no avail . . . my buyers made an alternative lodge purchase, and I licked my wounds and went back to looking for a March buyer.

In the next two months we showed the motel to a number of other prospects and by February there were two or three promising possibilities in the early stages of evaluation and negotiation. At that point I thought I'd better check out the mortgage situation with the Stowe bank (that had taken over the S.B.A. guaranteed loan), so that I could weigh the possibility of an assumption of the exiting mortgage or the availability of a new mortgage to a qualified buyer. Ushered into the bank manager's office, I explained the stage of my selling efforts and was shocked to my socks by her reaction. "Why, Bob, that place is under foreclosure by the S.B.A. The Smiths were way behind in their mortgage payments. The S.B.A. served papers on them nine months ago; the redemption period has run out, and the place is slated to be auctioned off in less than two weeks." I must have looked white as a ghost; I was astonished . . .

"Why, that place is doing fine and George has a good second income. There must be some mistake."

"No mistake," she said, "the S.B.A. has written acknowledgment that papers were served by a federal attorney."

Still in disbelief, I drove straight to the S.B.A. office in Montpelier. "No mistake," confirmed the S.B.A. officer. "They were served notice by our attorney back in September. We've scheduled an auction within two weeks of today!" Still reeling as evening approached, I drove next to the motel. There was a tour bus parked in front of the place and no one at the front desk, so I went down to the restaurant and found George, who happened to be in residence that weekend, cooking an early dinner for the bus arrivals. As calmly as I could manage, I said, "George, can you leave the kitchen for a few minutes . . . I must speak with you."

"C'mon Bob, can't you see I'm up to my elbows in a feeding operation here . . . come back in a couple of hours," was his reply.

"George, let me put it this way . . . you don't own that spatula in your hand and you don't own that range!" I had finally gotten his attention. He still peered at me like I was making some poor joke, but he could sense I was upset, so he took off his apron and stepped into the hall.

"George, this motel, lock, stock and spatula, is scheduled for public auction in two weeks." Time was of the essence and there was just no other way to break the news.

What had happened was a textbook case of procrastination and denial, complicated perhaps by a subconscious need by Estelle to create crisis and elicit a missing degree of attention from George. Many of us do comparable things like procrastinating on our income tax 'til we're in hot water, and denial is the keystone to many addictions, but in this case it was about to cost these good folks some $270,000. For, perhaps unjustifiably, there is no effort by the banks to repay any overage realized at an auction, so George and Estelle were within an ace of forfeiting the whole enchilada.

To make a long story short, I luckily had a friend who had formerly been an attorney for the U.S. Small Business Administration. He got us a hearing with the manager of the Vermont office, and after much mea culpa pleading, we were able to convince the S.B.A. that we could sell the place given two months grace period, and thus assure the S.B.A. of a more certain payment of the full mortgage loan than could be guaranteed by an auction.

With the blessing of providence, and with frantic, last-minute machinations to solve an unreported failed septic situation, deal with an in-house restaurant whose license had never been properly approved, bring outmoded fire prevention equipment up to code, etc., etc., we were able to sell the place to a couple from the West, rescue the Smiths from the squeeze play, and realize a reasonable price for the motel.

I've never been more exhausted or proud of my efforts and those of the attorney who stepped in on our behalf. Had we run into an inflexible bureaucrat at the S.B.A., the Smiths could have lost it all. But "all's well that ends well" . . . George and Estelle now have that dream home they've worked so hard to realize . . . and I'd been reminded that a crisis ignored just compounds itself. If you find yourself in a bind, don't let your embarrassment incapacitate you; tell someone, elicit their help, and there are usually good folks ready to help solve the problem.

"The Sign"

At the end of the RacePath

CHAPTER 24

Vermont has been the innovator of a number of environmental ideas that have worked to preserve our way of life. Ideas, that by being applied to all equally, have achieved their objectives without really diminishing our freedoms. One of these innovations was the country's first bottle deposit bill, which through a small monetary incentive, encouraged us to return and recycle bottles. This is further enhanced by the annual "Green-up Day" when kids from one to ninety-two (including the governor) get in their old clothes and pick-ups and scour the highways and by-ways picking up discarded trash and bottles. It's become a fun, family day, and while beautifying the countryside, enough 5-cent bottle deposits can be gleaned to buy lunch for the participants.

Another Vermont innovation is the sign law. No advertising signs are allowed along the interstates and other advertising signs are limited to on-premises with strict size limitations. It really has saved us from becoming a "Barnum & Bailey World." The Stowe Area Realtors have even agreed that no real estate "for-sale" signs will be used in our community. It has a wonderful over-all impact on visitors, and we still get the word out if a property is for sale.

I did have one situation where the state sign law appeared to put a developer in a disadvantageous position. He was subdividing a lovely wooded hillside area lying on the far side of the West Branch River. The sixty-five acre area had good gravel-road access, lovely woods and views, and large five acre parcels, but alas, it was situated about half a mile inboard from the Mountain Road. With the state prohibition against even an identifying sign "off-premises," there was no apparent way for my client to let all those wonderful prospects, driving up and down the access road to the ski areas, know that he had desirable property for sale. Then he came up with a very creative idea:

"Bob, would you go to all the neighbors of my land and then to the Town of Stowe and ask them if they would let me cover that bridge that leads over the West Branch River to my land?"

To put this situation in historical perspective, bridges were covered in the old days in Vermont because they were constructed of long log beams that spanned the stream covered by wooden planking. Because the snow and rain would eventually rot out the planks and beams, these bridges were covered with wooden superstructures having roofs to shield them from the freezing and melting elements.

So, naturally, when Bill made his suggestions I said, "But Bill, that's a contemporary concrete bridge, and covering it would have no practical purpose . . . or would it?" I had hardly voiced my objection when I realized that my bright friend was way ahead of me. The covered bridge would be his sign . . . and, naturally, he would name his development "The Covered Bridge Resort."

When I canvased them, the neighbors all thought he'd lost his marbles to waste thousands of dollars covering a concrete bridge, but they had no objection, nor did the town, so for about $25,000 he built a classical old post-and-beam cover over the bridge and it turned out to be, hands-down, the most effective sign in town. To this day, I don't think one person in a hundred knows that it's actually a modern covered bridge . . . but it looks attractive, adds to the old New England charm of the town, and is a very functional sign.

My postscript on the bridge was the lovely fall day I happened to be walking by the stream, and encountered a lady at her easel working on a painting of "the Old New England Covered Bridge." I tipped my hat, commented on the fine weather, and not wanting to rain on her parade, never said a word to the lady about the origin of her bridge.

Arnt Von Bohlen
und Halbach
1938 ~
↑
Alfried Krupp Von
Bohlen und Halbach
1907 ~ 1967
owner of fried. Krupp
↑
Bertha Krupp
1886 ~ 1957
owner of fried. Krupp
↑
Friedrich Alfred Krupp
1854 ~ 1902
owner of fried. Krupp

[from Geneology Chart]

"Wrap It Up, I'll Take It!"

Chapter 25

A handsome young lawyer dropped into the office one day, having been referred by a mutual friend. He was brimming with self-assurance and eager to find just the right situation for his "dream house." However, his definition was not very helpful:

"I don't know what I want but I'll know it when I see it, and price is a secondary consideration."

So with that wide latitude, we started looking at everything from luxury homes to log cabins. It was an exhaustive and exhausting search, but nothing seemed to quite fill the "dream." Then one evening I got a call from the young man . . . "I've found it; all you've got to do is get it listed, negotiate a price within reason, and you've made a sale."

Curiosity gripped me. "Where was this undiscovered gem?"

Well, it turned out to be a lovely little renovated antique schoolhouse on West Hill. I had to concur with the lawyer's taste. Albeit very modest in size and primitive in structure, it was a historic charmer.

Of course, I'd never heard of the place being for sale but my customer was saying he'd pay any reasonable price, so I optimistically scanned the town records to determine the location of the owner. The town clerk did volunteer, cryptically, that I might be wasting my time, but I persevered and found that a Mrs. Von Bohlen was the owner and that her current address was in West Germany.

I was still undeterred; I figured it must be expensive for her to carry this property in Stowe at arm's length with all the attendant taxes, insurance, and maintenance fees; maybe she'd be delighted to accept a generous offer and unburden herself of the financial drain. Therefore, armed with her address, I placed a call to Germany, reached a domestic in the household, and was advised to call back a couple of days later. I called my attorney friend to report on my efforts and he reiterated that he was prepared to pay a price that would motivate the lady to sell.

It just happened that I was joining my friend Dick Kruger for dinner that particular evening. Dick and I were engaged in our usual political and philosophical discussion when I spotted his most recent reading material. It was a book on the somewhat checkered fortunes of the Krupp dynasty. The Krupp's had supplied the Kaiser with munitions for the First World War, and again succumbed to Hitler's needs in re-arming Germany for the Second World War. But they had been for generations the dominant steel producing and fabricating family of the Ruhr Basin. Were they actually guilty with Hitler and his henchmen for the uses to which the Third Reich put their production? Or were they legitimate industrialists unaware at the outset of his dreams of world domination and racial genocide?

Whilst debating the issue, I leafed to the back of the book which contained a fold-out genealogical chart of the Krupp family. As I scanned the aristocratic German names, my eyes were suddenly riveted; there at the apex of the genealogical pyramid was the name . . . *Von Bohlen.*

Dick was surprised to see me almost rolling on the floor with laughter. Now I understood what the town clerk had been trying to tell me. I had been right on the verge of re-calling Mrs. Von Bohlen to tell her that, if she played her cards right, I might be able to get her as much as $150,000 for her modest little renovated schoolhouse . . . and free her from all those nagging carrying costs.

I did check it out further, but on firm advice from her caretaker that she could probably buy the whole town if she wanted, decided to save the cost of the phone call. In retrospect, perhaps I should at least have called again to see if I could have gotten past the butler.

"Poetic Justice"

Chapter 26

There happen to be very few black people in northern Vermont. Even though the "underground railway" in Civil War times reached up into Vermont, very few blacks have ever settled here. I guess the severe cold of our winters is not to the liking of most people of partially African ancestry.

One day, a very handsome young black man walked into our Stowe office looking for a parcel of land on which to eventually build a vacation home. He was an "on-location" reporter for the Public Broadcasting System; quite a prestigious job. He and my partner drove over the countryside and fairly quickly decided on a lovely, two-acre parcel on the Elmore Mt. Road in a subdivision that had been developed by Bill Murphy.

But by the time the soils had passed state-required testing, and the title vetted, Rodney Ward, our black customer, was on location in New Orleans. He insisted he wanted to close in person and called from several locations around the nation, but he kept requesting delays, and in the end he never did show up to tender his money and accept a deed. My partner, Kirby, finally asked me what he should do and I said, "Look, he's a black man and minorities can run into some insincere shuffles in the real estate world, so I suggest we bend over backwards to make him know we're sincere in offering to sell him this property. Let's record his sales agreement in the Elmore town clerk's office and give him another six months to get his act together and perform."

Well, Rodney never did show up again. We saw him on T.V. a couple of times, but we never did see him back in Stowe, so we finally sent his deposit back and forgot all about the deal.

Shortly thereafter, a more dire thing happened to Bill Murphy. The high-interest squeeze of '77, coupled with the delaying red-tape of Vermont's multiplicitous environmental laws, so hamstrung the development process that his subdivision was foreclosed upon by the bank. The bank simply took all the lots back that hadn't been sold. I felt great sympathy for Bill, 'cause he had worked so hard, and "hung in there" responsibly for his people to the bitter end, but finally he had to fold his tent and head back to his former media business in New York. Fortunately Bill and his talented wife, Kathie, were able to pick up the pieces and once again flourish in the New York ad business, but the land development process had been very costly to them in time and money and disappointment.

Then, about four years after the foreclosure, I happened to be in the Elmore clerk's office checking on the resale of the bank's lots when I discovered a curious thing. According to the records, Lot #2 had never been taken back by the bank. It didn't seem to make sense, so I asked the town clerk about the current ownership of that lot. "Oh, the bank didn't include that one lot in their foreclosure, because there was a recorded sales agreement in the records to Rodney S. Ward, and they didn't want to chance any controversy."

"Well, who does own it?" I persisted.

"Actually it seems to be in limbo; the bank doesn't own it, Rodney Ward doesn't own it, and Mr. Murphy's development corporation is defunct as far as we know. There's three years' back taxes due and we're about to auction it off in a couple of weeks."

In actual practice, very few people are ever aware of such actions, so my first reaction was, "Hey, for about $400 in back taxes, I can own a beautiful two-acre parcel with stunning views on the Elmore Mt. Road." Then, unfortunately, my more empathetic conscience gripped me and I said to myself, "Naw, this is poetic justice; for a mere $400 Bill Murphy can recoup at least one piece of the property he worked so hard to develop."

So I called Bill in New York, informed him of the situation, and with great appreciation, he put through a resolution legally re-establishing the defunct corporation for one day, sent his check for $400 to the town clerk, and now owns at least a little slice of Vermont. He cherishes the symbolism of the land, and although we've since sent him offers that have escalated to $42,000 for that property, he says it just isn't for sale for love nor money.

I don't know where Rodney Ward is these days. I hope he's doing well in television. I'm sure he did intend to buy that land, but just got too "other-directed." Yet we can thank him for having played a propitious role in Bill Murphy's life.

"Ditties"

Courtesy of Glenn Moody

Chapter 27

Until recently, in the recreational areas of northern Vermont, real estate activity could be very seasonal. There was often a need to supplement one's income through other activities. My vehicle was to revert to entertaining at various lodges. One winter I sang at the Trapp Family Lodge atop Luce Hill in Stowe. As the Trapps were famous singers in their own right, I always felt like I was "carrying coals to Newcastle", but Johannes Von Trapp, who is a very gracious man, offered to pay me a reasonable wage and let me set my own schedule; so it was too good to pass up.

One night I was entertaining the crowd in the bar when one of the guests commented, "You sing so beautifully." I beamed with satisfaction, when the bartender added, "You ought to see him ski, lady."

But before I could savor the compliment, Bernie Stasiak, down the bar, chimed in, "Yeah, but he's a lousy lover." Bernie had adroitly burst my balloon, but he also gave me a natural lead line for a ditty set to simple guitar chords:

"DITTIES"

Verse
He could ski like Jean Killy, emote like a Hollywood star.
Close your eyes, you'd swear it's Segovia
When he picks up his guitar.
His looks would eclipse Robert Redford.
His estates are of jet-set renown.
But when he unveils his pitch to the frails,
He comes off like an unemployed clown.

Refrain
For he's a lousy lover; some fellows are just cursed that way.
He'll wine them and dine them and then Gertrude Stein them,
But they'll never end up in the hay.
With a girl he will get so excited, stutter and sputter and fume:
When the candles, martinis, and supper are laid,
That's all that gets laid in his room.

Verse
But at last he was made ski instructor.
With ladies this never has failed.
When these Adonises pole down the mountain,
Countless damsels' hearts are impaled.
But Kerr made him turn in his parka.
He'd brought dishonor on Stowe.
Three girls from his classes, with magnificent chassis
Survived pure as the driven snow.

Refrain
For he's a lousy lover, his ineptitude spread far and wide.
The girls often fell for the No-tell Motel.
But he'll fall on his face once inside.
Yes, he's a lousy lover; the moral is plain there to see.
'Tis better to master the lessons of love 'ere the stage,
The guitar and the ski.

Then, en route to the state real estate convention one year, my companion commented that, as I seemed to have a knack for dashing off musical ditties, why didn't I contribute a bit of doggerel extolling the virtues of the intrepid real estate agent. So as we drove along, I let a few rhymes develop in my mind and delivered the following to the assembled group that evening:

He's the thrivin', connivin', hard-bargain-drivin' real estate man
He'll get you to sign the dotted line as fast as he can.
But his golden retirement estates are just quicksand and rattlesnakes
'Cause he's the thrivin', connivin', hard-bargain-drivin' real estate man.

He'd sell you the Brooklyn Bridge if he thought you'd buy it.
The house comes equipped with a fridge, but don't bother to try it
The pond site's just a miasmic swamp; the well is dry but the basement's damp.

"DITTIES"

And if you read him the ad, this cad will completely deny it.

Or he'll sell you a country retreat, replete with seclusion.
When you get there, you meet with the noise of the street and confusion.
How can you relax and enjoy your camp, when the front door opens on a freeway ramp?
Your dream of seclusion was just this realtor's illusion

'Cause he's the thrivin', connivin', hard-bargain-drivin' real estate man.
He'll get you to sign the dotted line as fast as he can.
But his golden retirement estates are just quicksand and rattlesnakes
He's the thrivin', connivin', hard-bargain-drivin' real estate man.

My efforts were received in good humor by the assembled Real estate establishment except for those inevitable few who take themselves too seriously. I was also aware that "real estate person" would have been more appropriate as more than half the brokers in Vermont were women . . . but it just didn't scan.

A potential boon to us Vermont Realtors are the tourists who come to visit our fair state for a week or a weekend and then find they're reluctant to leave this Garden of Eden. Sometimes they'll leave, sadly looking forward to next year's visit, but some find themselves looking for a Vermont vacation home, and still others start seeking a way to make a living in Vermont or to move their business here.

With the advent of the computer age, many entrepreneurs find they can work out of their Vermont homes abetted by computers and fax machines with sporadic visits to the markets where their services or products are marketed. Remembering how I felt when I had to leave Vermont after a ski trip, I put some blues chords to the following:

I got those Sunday evenin' rear-vision-mirror blues.
I'm leaving Stowe, all this snow, and a gal I can't afford to lose.
How can I hold her affection; drivin' three hundred miles in the wrong direction
While some ski pro steps into my shoes?

City livin's about to break my mind.
Kind words there are getting rare, I find.
But if I could just make the break
This weary little bod I'd take
Back to Stowe, all that snow.
Fresh air affection I'd infuse
Where I can stow these rear-vision-mirror blues.

In 1980, my fellow realtor, Barbara Williams, called to suggest that the Whip, the bar at the venerable old Green Mountain Inn in Stowe Village, needed entertainment.

"DITTIES"

The original Green Mountain Inn had been a massive hotel serviced by the stagecoach trade from New York, Boston, Albany, and other eastern cities. In 1889 it burned down and in 1893 the present inn was built. As the wife of a more recent owner, Parker Perry, had the maiden name of Whipple, he decided to call the bar and lounge The Whip. Accordingly the theme of the decor of the place is a great collection of historical buggy whips.

Parker Perry was a rather egotistical character who loved to play the curmudgeon. He could be singularly inhospitable, but the visitors from the cities found him so quaint and inimitable that they not only tolerated but seemed to enjoy his superior attitude and mild put-downs. In addition, he considered himself a word-smith rivaling William F. Buckley. He delighted in throwing out sesquipedalian responses to the queries of his guests. In short, he was such a colorful, independent character that I couldn't resist penning the following ditty, which I sang at his bar whenever he was absent. I inverted his names just to stay on the safe side of the laws of defamation:

In Perry Parker's Blue Mountain Inn,
The most amazin' place you've ever been,
Where the furniture's antique, and the mattresses all squeak,
You've gotta tiptoe down the hall to find the relief you seek.

Now Perry's not the world's most genial fellow,

But your genealogy he'll not demean.
He cares not if you're black or white or yellow.
Just pay your hotel bill in tender green.
Now the Whip has drinks at prices realistic.
But the waiters there get madder by the hour
'Cause the decor is so sado-masochistic,
And the house drink is a Torquemada Sour.

(Repeat refrain)

Perry's oft abstruse alliteration
Hides a disdain for pedantic lexicon.
He much prefers to eschew obfuscation
At least until the common folks have gone.

And Perry's use of space is very frugal:
There's a bed in every nook and cranny there.
That's why a mountain guide equipped with bugle
Will lead you to your castle in mid-air.

In Perry Parker's Blue Mountain Inn,
The most amazin' place you've ever been.
But the service there's so slow
That I'm still waitin' for Godot
In Perry Parker's Blue Mountain Inn.

In Stowe's earlier skiing years, back in the '40s, '50s, and '60s, so-called release bindings on skis were pretty primitive. They were so unresponsive to the impact of a fall on the mountain, that they were known as bear traps. The only orthopedic surgeon in the area in those days was Dr. David Bryan. On a busy Saturday afternoon in ski season, there would be a line in Dr. Bryan's office awaiting X-rays, diagnosis, and plaster, as he set the broken limbs. It could be a virtual plaster assembly line.

Thanks to his thriving practice, Dr. Bryan built the largest house then in Stowe Hollow. Ironically the next biggest house in Stowe Hollow belonged to Bob Meyers who just happened to own The Village Ski Shop, where most of the ski bindings were sold and adjusted. I got thinking about this coincidence and wondered whether collusion could have contributed to the mutual well-being of these two neighbors. My lyrics just happened to fit neatly into the tune of Tennessee Ernie Ford's Sixteen Tons:

I awoke one morning; it was drizzling rain.
I picked up my poles and I lay down my cane.
I made sixteen runs on the icy slopes.
Now my leg still moves, but on pulleys and ropes.

You make sixteen runs and what-da-ya get?
   Another day older and another bone set.
   St. Peter, don't call me 'cause I can't go:
   I owe my soul to the doctor at Stowe.

Now, if you see me comin', you'd better ski aside.
A lotta cats didn't and a lotta cats died.

The skis are Heads but the skier's a heel.
If the right one don't get ya, then the left one will.

   Repeat of refrain . . . then.
Now according to Bob Meyers' latest independent findings
Skiing's safer than walking with the new release bindings.
But through collusions and contusions the top mansions in Stowe
Belong to Meyers and a certain Dr. Bryan we know.

   You make sixteen runs and what-da-ya get?
   Another day older and another bone set.
   St. Peter, don't call me 'cause I can't go:
   I owe my soul to the doctor of Stowe.

   I hasten to add that my lightly veiled accusation was with tongue in cheek, because Dr. Bryan was a friend who really got me started in real estate. He had accumulated large tracts of northern Vermont land as many farms went fallow and were put into tree farms with the aid of a governmental program. Dr. Bryan had bought all this land at minimal prices. He didn't try to maximize his good fortune and when he sold the land it was at very reasonable prices employing me as his agent. I walked every acre of his far-flung tracts and found buyers who wanted to get in on the ground floor of Vermont's early land appreciation.
   The sad note is that we kept missing connections and I

never got to sing the song for my friend, Dave Bryan, before his untimely death. Knowing Dave, I'm sure he'd have secretly enjoyed it.

"Vignettes"

POST OFFICE
MOSCOW, VT. 05662

CHAPTER 28

"Moscow, Vermont"

One little valley hamlet within Stowe is known as Moscow, VT. It even boasts its own U.S. Post Office in DeCelle's General Store. The generally accepted explanation of the origin of the name is that back in the 1800s when the dinner bells all sounded at once in the little valley or when Adams Mill banged on the huge old saw blade they used as a bell, it was reminiscent of the cathedral bells of Moscow that all rang simultaneously when Napoleon's army was repulsed by the Russians in 1812.

A few people still maintain that the name was a homophone for "Ma's Cow," but in any case, the name is sure an attention-getter for a place so absolutely remote from the capital of Russia.

The name did cost me a potential sale. I was showing a Hungarian lady various sites around Stowe for a land investment when I recalled an ideal five-acre parcel for her purposes. We went to see it, and she was close to signing a contract, when I added that she'd also have her own quaint mailing address . . . Moscow, VT. "No," she said in a heavy east European accent, "I will not own land in Moscow." Unfortunately for me, the time was just after Hungary was crushed by Russian tanks in their first abortive attempt to break with the Soviets. The lady could not be dissuaded from her position . . . Moscow was off limits and so was my sale.

Ironically, things have now changed so drastically in Eastern Europe and the Soviet Union that in 1989 we had a visit by Russian students to Stowe. My favorite photo in the Stowe Reporter showed a line up of young Russians sending postcards home to Leningrad from the Moscow General Store; what a difference a decade makes.

Moscow, VT has one other claim to fame. Each July 4th at 10 a.m. they have their own Independence Day Parade. All the locals turn out in Spirit of '76 regalia, but in lieu of a marching band, all the Moscow Village houses turn up the volume on their radios, open their windows wide, and WRFB (Stowe) plays John Philip Sousa marches for that designated hour. It's a truly splendid bit of Americana and has even been covered by Charles Kuralt and the CBS News.

"The Diaspora Revisited"

Real estate sales in a recreational area of Vermont can bring a wide variety of customers and friends one's way. I'd been fortunate to meet a charming Egyptian gentleman from New York who was, at the time, Attaché for

Tourism from the United Arab Republic under Gabdel Nassar's regime. Ironically his name was Nassar A. Nassar (no relation to the head of state). My friend Nassar was writing a book, and asked if he could sojourn at my little Vermont farmhouse for a few days, in hopes that the Vermont ambiance would help the flow of his creative juices. He had no sooner arrived for the long, early-spring weekend when Alan Rudner, a land client of mine, called from Montreal to ask if he could stay at my house for some late season skiing that weekend. I responded that he was also welcome with the reservation that he, a Jewish Canadian, would have to share my only guest bedroom with an Arab.

Alan thought the situation fraught with humorous irony which might even promote the cause of world peace, so the arrangement was agreed upon by both parties. Then, as fate would have it, another local client of mine called bemoaning the fact that the sister of his current hot-and-heavy romantic flame was arriving in town and threatening to put a major crimp in his love life . . . could Pat Flynn's sister Kelly share my humble abode Saturday night and place her sleeping bag on my living room floor. To his surprise, I quickly agreed, for I now realized we could have a Moslem, a Jew, a Catholic, and a Protestant all living under the same roof . . . and this happened to be Palm Sunday weekend, rather big on the calendar of all the faiths represented.

As you might imagine, we had much good-natured by-play about the comparative merits of our religions culminating in my suggestion at Sunday morning breakfast that we all attend Palm Sunday service at the Episcopal church. After quips about our group presence threatening the structural integrity of the church building, all finally agreed it would be an historic first in little Stowe, VT.

Then The Lord quite mysteriously frustrated our ecumenical outing. Inexplicably, after working well for fifteen years, the hammer in my front-door lock sprung in such a way that the door could not be opened. As the house had no other door at that time and the storm windows were affixed from the outside, we couldn't leave the house until we had sawn through the lock hammer with a hacksaw . . . by the time we'd freed the door, it was too late to make church service and the diaspora was preserved. To this day Alan thinks Jehovah didn't want this motley crew darkening His doors. Perhaps 'tis true, "the Lord works in mysterious ways."

"The Two Norman Keiths"

By unique coincidence, I once had to write letters to two different Norman Keiths in the same week. The first Norman Keith was the, then, Chairman of the Board of Continental Oil Company . . . I was in the process of selling his vacation home on Spruce Peak adjacent to the Mountain and I was very much impressed by this board room general.

The second Norman Keith was a diary farmer on the

Elmore Mountain Road to whom I'd leased some extra land in the area. I would say that he was a prime example of the elemental Vermont rustic. I really did have to be careful which letter went in which envelope (like a college kid with two sweethearts), because the worlds of these two gentlemen couldn't have been more disparate.

The irony is that in the eighteen intervening years since mailing those letters, the U.S. oil business has suffered substantial setbacks, whereas 400 acres of prime land on the Elmore Mountain Road, with all its panoramic views, has virtually exploded in value. Could well be that, today, Norman Keith, the "poor dairy farmer," has a greater net worth than Norman Keith, the oil mogul. Life sure does present some twists and turns . . . as my friend says, "be kind to your secretary, tomorrow she may be your boss."

"Falling in Love with an Aura"

In the haunting classic movie, "Laura," played by Gene Tierney, the detective, played by Dana Andrews, is assigned to study the home and effects of the alluring and mysterious "Laura" who is missing and presumed dead. In the process, he becomes obsessed by the aura, beauty, and mystique of his subject: the scent of her perfume, the choice of her decor; the words of her letters; the recording of her voice; and the haunting portrait of the beautiful Laura over the fireplace. As his investigation develops he becomes infatuated with the pieced-together vestiges of his subject. He has fallen in love with a woman he's never met.

When it turns out that Laura is still alive after all, the plot thickens and romance blossoms.

The same obsession seized me when I listed Kathy Hubbard's home in Duxbury years ago. She had heard of me and had sent me a lovely letter of introduction, a listing on her house, and a key, suggesting that I familiarize myself with the place in her absence.

The choice of words in her letter had already had an impact, but when I let myself into her house, I found myself becoming preoccupied with her photo, her books, her perfume, her taste in clothes. There was a unique aura of charm and taste. Over her bed, I found a sign that read, "Make Love, Not War," and I found myself feeling jealousy for whoever may have shared that bed with her. I actually didn't want to leave the place; I almost had to drag myself away.

I imagine it happens to other realtors from time to time, both men and women. We do get an intimate look into a person's way of life and I imagine there are liaisons that have begun even before the parties actually have met. In Kathy's case, when I finally did meet her face to face, the reality was everything the house and my imagination had conjured and I think perhaps she was also impacted . . . but alas, she was involved with another man, and I didn't have the chutzpa to pursue my instinct. I'm still haunted by the memory sometimes, and reminded that "the saddest words of mouth or pen are these, my friend, it might have been."

"Three Hundred Dollars a Word"

Verner Z. Reed was a wealthy and rather eccentric young man whose estate lied at the head of Sterling Valley. Verner had enough money to be able to "march to a different drummer" and to get away with foibles that might have brought a lesser or poorer man acropper. On his estate, he had a wonderful collection of vehicles and machines, playthings that only he could afford. He also had a lovely, 45-acre parcel of woodland not contiguous to his home place.

Arthur Shulman, a Canadian customer of mine, became quite desirous of Verner's woodlot. I told Art that Verner was highly unlikely to sell the piece and certainly didn't need the money, but Art was an aggressive gentleman and insisted that we drop in on Verner to test the waters. Art had a particularly attractive wife and, on the morning of our impromptu visit, I think we caught Verner in a moment of weak resistance and strong libido. To my surprise, almost before I knew what had happened, Art and Verner came to a verbal agreement on the purchase of the 45 acres, and I drew up a letter of intent on the spot for Art's purchase.

However, by the next morning, quite predictably, Verner was on the phone to me repudiating his letter and reneging on any sale of his property. Unfortunately for Verner, Arthur was a tough Montreal attorney, and wasn't willing to accept this change of heart lying down. He started making sounds like . . . "damages . . . lawsuits for specific performance, etc." Verner was not in the least intimidated and, with good legal advice, would probably have been able to cite several flaws in the impromptu letter that offered escape from the deal. However, as he was not used to having to play by conventional rules, and in reaction to Mr. Shulman's pressure, he simply sent a letter which read:

Dear Mr. Shulman:
With all due respect, may I suggest that you "go shit in your hat."
                                    Very truly yours,
                                    Verner Z. Reed, 3rd

A masterpiece of succinctness if I ever saw one, but the upshot was that in an out-of-court settlement, the letter cost Mr. Reed exactly $300 per word. I guess if one is sufficiently well heeled, $300 a word might be justified by the pleasure of venting one's spleen so graphically. As for the rest of us, we'd best be careful of the sentiments we put in writing . . . particularly the expletives undeleted.

"What's a Bathing Suit?"

I grew up in an era when there was a greater emphasis on personal modesty than there is today. Perhaps the young people of today are just more open and less hypocritical than we were in the '40s, '50s, and '60s.

I was showing land in the Gregg Hill area to a couple of very appealing young women a few years back. It was a 57-acre parcel of variable terrain, and by the time we'd walked every inch of it, we were scratched, bedraggled, and overheated. They thanked me for my time and promised they'd give the land serious consideration, and then asked how close we were to the Waterbury Reservoir. I was happy to tell them that it could be accessed by a trail about half a mile down the Gregg Hill road.

The reservoir is a gorgeous, pristine, secluded body of water that fills in about seven miles of the Little River Valley now that the government has built a massive dam at the end of the valley as part of a water control project.

I told the young women more about the reservoir and its relative privacy and they said it was a perfect place to go swimming after our arduous land inspection. Generously they offered, "Why don't you join us?"

"Gee, I'd love to," I replied, "but I don't have a bathing suit."

"What's a bathing suit?" was Jane's rejoinder.

I really didn't have an adequate response to that question, so off we went to the reservoir.

They were every bit as attractive in the altogether as I'd imagined, and the swim was fun, titillating, exciting . . . and unfortunately, quite innocent. I think the only embarrassed member of the trio was me. We've come a long way since Lady Godiva's ride!

"Romania"

One person who elicited my special ongoing efforts in her land search was a striking young damsel from Massachusetts who I met at the Sans Souci Lodge. In addition to being a serious prospect, she was a fine skier and an intelligent, ash-blond charmer. Happily, our relationship developed into more than that of realtor/customer.

Patty had one rather unique foible. Her lineage was part Romanian, and although she had let that fact slip out in an unguarded moment, she was in strong denial of that part of her genealogy. I guess it was partly because of the myth that some Romanians are thieving peripatetic gypsies who are wont to emanate from that southeastern European area. I'm sure in many cases the Gypsies get a bad rap: Carlos Montoya, the distinguished flamenco guitarist, claims Gypsy lineage and is very proud of it.

At first, I kidded Patty about this sensitivity, but soon found that to be counter productive to our growing friendship and deftly avoided the subject.

At any rate, our relationship was going swimmingly until one evening we stopped into the Grand Motor Inn on the Mountain Road. We found ourselves facing a large round table of Stowe's expatriate European skiers;

fellows from all over the Austrian and Carpathian Alps. Oscar was from Czechoslovakia, Bernie was from Poland, Ted was from Hungary, Milos was from Yugoslavia, etc. Stowe's challenging skiing has always drawn some of the best of these European emigrés.

I spontaneously commented on the fascinating United Nations representation at the table, and then made the fatal faux pas of adding that, appropriately, Patty was from Romania. As soon as I said it, I tried to retrieve my words, but before I could change the subject Bernie said,

"Then you must know how to make a Romanian omelet."

Patty stiffened and demurred, but Bernie went on to explain that *"first you have to steal a dozen eggs."*

Unable to curb my laughter, I realized that I had just witnessed the beginning of the end of a potential land sale and a lovely relationship.

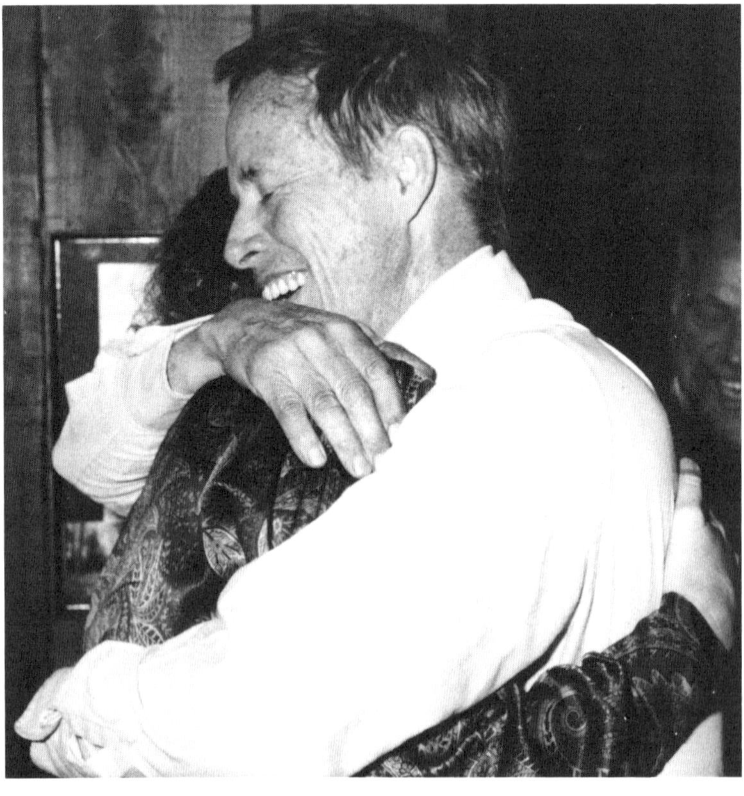

"When Is Enough"

Chapter 29

One of life's most profound questions, when saving for a rainy day or planning for retirement is, "when is enough." I guess we could pose the question in regard to religion or power or success or even lovemaking . . . "when is enough." But the question is most obvious when we apply it to that nest egg which will give us enough security to leave the arena, (where we compete for the almighty dollar) and capture the time to smell the flowers or pursue those creative talents that we've long subordinated to earning a living.

Of course, the luckiest among us are those who have had the guts or the fortune to follow their "bliss" (as Joseph Campbell would put it) from the outset; those who were able to subordinate the making of money to joyfully pursuing the God-given talent with which they were endowed.

Years ago, I met a man in Wilton, Conn., whose luxurious estate impressed me less than his air, at the age of 66, of joy and equanimity. I felt compelled to ask him what his secret had been in achieving both financial success and a rare degree of serenity. He explained that when he got out of college, he figured that if he worked very hard on Wall Street for 45 years, he'd be able to retire at 65 and pursue his great love, which was boats . . . so he figured, "Why don't I just start joyfully working on boats right now?"

In effect, he thus, retired at 20 and started working in a boat yard. Of course, he started out making a pittance, but he loved it so much and spent so much time at it that he eventually made a great success doing what he loved to do . . . and never had to retire again. For some lucky few, real estate is so fascinating as to be the equivalent of that boat yard. To others it's a daily struggle.

Beset by life's responsibilities, very few of us are secure enough to throw caution to the wind and travel the route of our "true bliss." We compromise by finding an activity which will use some of our talents; a work which we can enjoy about 37% of the time and which will guarantee a paycheck to meet the mortgage payments. Then having pursued that compromise for 35 to 45 years, and having put some money aside as we went along, we arrive back at the question, "when is enough."

I remember when I was struggling to cope with the high pressure TV business in New York. I said to myself, "If I ever have $25,000 free and clear, I'll quit this rat-race and write music and work in the woods and ski and . . ." Then, as I became vested in the profit-sharing plan, it became . . . "If I ever get $50,000 ahead . . . if I ever get $100,000 . . . if I ever get . . ." And that can go on, ad infinitum, until our health and youth are gone and we're sitting in front of a large screen TV set hugging our million dollar stock portfolio and wondering where all the time and dreams went. Kahlil Gibran said, "What is a man's thirst when his well is full, but the thirst which is unquenchable" . . . and other sages have urged, "Carpe diem," seize the day . . . and Jesus said, "What profiteth a man if he gain the whole world and lose his own life."

Yes, we all tend to promise ourselves, "As soon as I've made these last few real estate deals . . . as soon as I've solved these last few major problems . . . then I'll allow myself the luxury to savor the true essence of life." The rub is, those last few deals or last few problems that stand between us and the true participation in our talents and bliss are like the dotted lines in a rolling highway. We look ahead and see those next twenty dotted segments to be dealt with, but when we get up ahead, the lines keep going on . . . forever!

Furthermore, if I've learned anything, it's that there's no amount of money that gives security; even security about money. We can scrimp and save for a lifetime, and have our nest-egg knocked out by one act of Congress or one illness. There'll never be enough . . . (when Ivana and the banks are through, Donald Trump may not even have enough). So unless we're one of those fortunate few whose job is also his joy and artistic fulfillment, we'd better decide when is enough and then have the guts and discipline to get up from the poker table; pocket our modest winnings; turn our back on the last big deal; and start pursuing those things that truly fulfill us.

Real Estate is uniquely hard to conclude; i.e. real estate transactions always leap-frog one another. There is never a moment when we can say all our current involvement is concluded, and there's always that one last big closing in the sky.

However, with much agonizing and many false "retirements," I finally decided that December 1, 1989 would be my "swan song," while I could still ski and work in my beloved woods, and maybe even belatedly court a woman. And my situation was further accentuated by a physical exam wherein the woman doctor had summed up my condition by stating, "You're in remarkable shape . . . but, let's face it, you're not right off the showroom floor."

So I decided to slowly fade into the woods and woodwork. I resigned my few exclusive listings; I quietly cleaned out my office and moved to an obscure desk; and actually discussed my real estate demise with very few people. (Nor did many people comment on my passing.) I obviously wasn't a major factor anymore in the new, faster-moving, multiple-listing world of real estate. The general lack of comment on the street about my withdrawal just confirmed my decision to bow out. "Sic transit gloria mundi."

So, on November 30th at 5:30 p.m., I was working up on the "Murray Memorial Park" clearing brush and burning when a young client, Nelson Russell, stopped by and located me by the firelight. To my embarrassment, he reminded me that we had a date to work out the final form of protective covenants on some land we had earlier put under contract. Naturally, I dropped what I was doing and in my sooty work clothes accompanied him back to the office where we spent the next hour hammering out acceptable restrictions to the use of the land.

When we'd concluded our work, I suggested that he join me for a beer or coffee at the "Flying Tomato." He agreed to join me if I wouldn't mind picking up his lovely wife, Marie, along the way. She was delivering brochures for her riding school to the lodges on Edson Hill, so figuring the timing of the delivery route, we calculated to catch up with her about halfway up Edson Hill in the vicinity of the Logwood Inn.

By the time we arrived at the Logwood, it was snowing heavily, but Nelson spotted Marie's car, so we pulled in and entered the foyer. Marie was there to greet us, but I was somewhat taken aback because, over Marie's shoulder, I could see a party was taking place involving some people I knew; a party to which I had obviously not been invited. I guess my immediate pang of hurt was a natural reaction; we've all felt pointedly "left out" at times.

"Oh well, you can't make 'em all," so I started to turn for the door when a flashbulb popped and a camcorder started to roll . . . and OH, MY GOD, THE PARTY'S FOR ME! I was absolutely dumbstruck; I could hardly grasp the situation. Here were 120 people including friends I hadn't seen in years. How could all this have been in preparation without leaking in a small tight-knit community.

I guess I've never been so surprised and pleased in my life. I think I hugged everyone in the room . . . both men and women. For me, it was the equivalent of all those closings over the years . . . and it was worth all the blood, sweat, and tears expended in trying to be honest and fair in my dealings with these people. At a time like this, money suddenly seems very unimportant.

When I had wiped away some tears and finished hugging everyone, I made a last turn toward an alcove where my imposing friend Duncan Nash stepped aside and there stood Fiona Strong, my friend from England, smashingly handsome and dripping with British breeding. Once again, I could hardly believe my eyes. I had been trying to lure this lady to America for years without success, but Sherry Wilson and Duncan, these cohorts of mine, had ransacked my desk, found her address, called her on the phone, and convinced her to abandon a very busy schedule to make a 6,000 mile round trip for a one-evening celebration.

She made a great contrast to the rustic, old Logwood Inn in her tailored, brass-buttoned, navy blue suit. I was so proud to have my friends meet her and confirm that she wasn't a figment of my imagination after all . . . and I was so proud to have her meet all my friends. What a fitting climax to such a stunning surprise.

Then:
— When I had read all the telegrams and opened all the presents;
— when I had been thoroughly "roasted" with the incisive exposure of my many idiosyncrasies by the assembled group; when I had been made to swear that I would never compete with them again;

— when I had danced 'til my wallet was wet; and
— when my dear friends had left, I finally sat down to the full realization that my real estate race had been run and that I'd been blessed in knowing instinctively, "when was enough." Now wonderful new episodes could evolve in my life . . . "maybe I'll even try to write a book."

Health problems were different in that the standards to be achieved were international rather than British. So the question of cultural superiority was not relevant. Obviously British methods and British training were resorted to, but not with the cultural overtones of education. Yet British health experts, like their fellow educators, probably erred by not paying enough attention to indigenous medicine, witch doctors and tribal cures. Empire health in the 1940s — as with political, economic and educational preparation — could not ask for acclaim on the grounds of an imperial trust well fulfilled, but the 1939—45 war brought a variety of new health initiatives; healthy soldiers were more efficient than unhealthy ones. So the campaigns for public health were stepped up, against malaria in west Africa, venereal disease in the West Indies, leprosy in Nigeria.

After the 1940 development and welfare legislation was passed, more funds were available from Britain for the extension of health services and for research into tropical health. Attention also began to focus on preventive and social medicine, on deficiency diseases and problems of diet, on the provision of welfare services such as maternity clinics. A royal commission investigating the conditions of the West Indies revealed in 1945 a great shortage of trained personnel, nurses as well as medical officers, and it urged that more medical training be carried out locally rather than overseas.[14] Overall, the West Indies was faring better in health than Africa and most other parts of the empire but even so conditions were much worse there than in the more developed countries. Barbados was among the healthiest of the West Indies islands but its infant mortality rate was four times that of Britain.

After 1945 health developments moved rapidly in an array of special projects, such as mosquitoes and malaria in Mauritius, yaws in the Pacific, sleeping sickness in Nigeria; tuberculosis was an empire-wide problem; leprosy was still widespread; hospital-building and medical training were given prime attention; problems of nutrition and food distribution were studied; town planning, sanitation and housing were improved.[15] The British government contributed funds to these schemes but perhaps more importantly undertook a vast training scheme for doctors, technicians and nurses from developing countries. Commonwealth scholarships were also provided for higher medical training and a commonwealth medical conference was set up to discuss common problems. Equally important was the research carried on by various British bodies, such as the London School of Hygiene and Tropical Medicine or the Institute of Parasitology in Cambridge; the inter-war years had seen a proliferation of such research and advisory bodies. The British government also worked in cooperation with international health bodies such as the World Health Organization.

As rapid as the advances were, it was obvious that the backlog could never be fully made up. For example, in 1965 Britain had one doctor for every 950 people while Malawi had only one for every 60,000; Britain had one trained nurse for every 500 patients while Ceylon had only one for every 3,780; Britain had 27 medical schools, commonwealth Africa only 5.[16] At the same time, health standards were showing a marked improvement, and this became clearly reflected in population growth rates, indeed to the extent that the charge could now be made that more efficient and extensive health services were creating a new problem, overpopulation. This has become serious in some Pacific islands, Western Samoa and Tonga, and is creating a land shortage. The obvious next step is education on birth control and land usage.

The mutation of the commonwealth-empire of 1940 into the commonwealth of the 1970s has been accompanied by many changes in attitudes. The coloured people of the empire lost their sense of subservience and resentment, and asserted instead a bold and vigorous sense of integrity and independence. At the same time the older dominions were also going through a phase of increased nationalism; emotional bonds with the "mother country" were weakening and new friends being found. The British government and people were developing a massive conscience about their imperial role and the possible evils that they had inflicted in the past on their colonial charges. So development became the essential theme, and development primarily for the benefit of the dependent people. But in all cases development came late, almost too late, and there was insufficient time, money and planning to complete the preparations thoroughly.

With these changes came an erosion of Britain's sense of cultural superiority; increasingly British planners accepted that initiative must pass to local hands, and full respect be given to local cultures. Britain might offer an example but as the years passed most of the new leaders chose to reject more and more the British way, relying partly on traditional influences but turning also to other foreign examples, both western and eastern, both capitalist and socialist. The breakdown of British cultural superiority also flowed through to the white dominions which in particular had to reassess the position of the indigenous peoples still living within their borders.

NOTES

1. John D. B. Miller, *Britain and the Old Dominions* (London: Chatto & Windus, 1966), pp. 236—38.
2. W. A. de Klerk, *The Puritans in Africa* (Harmondsworth: Penguin, 1975); earlier — G. H. Le May, *British Supremacy in South Africa, 1899—1907* (Oxford: Clarendon, 1965); L. M. Thompson, *The Unification of South Africa, 1902—10* (Oxford: Clarendon, 1960).
3. Keith Sinclair, "Why are Race Relations in New Zealand Better than in South Africa, South Australia or South Dakota?", *New Zealand Journal of History* 5 (1971): 121—27; Alice J. Metge, *The Maoris of New Zealand* (London: Routledge, Kegan, 1967); Eric Schwimmer, *The World of the Maori* (Wellington: Reed, 1966).

4. Gwendolyn Carter, *The Politics of Inequality* rev.ed. (New York: Praeger, 1959) Mary Benson, *The Struggle for a Birthright* (Harmondsworth: Penguin, 1966); Janet Robertson, *Liberalism in South Africa, 1948—63* (Oxford: Clarendon, 1971).
5. Colin Leys, *European Politics in South Rhodesia* (Oxford: Clarendon, 1959); Robert C. Good, *UDI* (London: Faber & Faber, 1974).
6. For example, see Derek Ingram, *Commonwealth for a Colour Blind World* (London: Allen & Unwin, 1965).
7. "Report of the Commission on Higher Education in West Africa", [Cmd.6655], *Parl.Pap.* 5 (1944—45): 593, at 20—25; for education figures, also see annual *Colonial Office List*; William K. Hancock, *Survey of British Commonwealth Affairs* (London: Oxford University Press, 1942), 2, part 2 is also useful. Re Gold Coast, Philip Foster, *Education and Social Change in Ghana* (London: Routledge & Kegan Paul, 1965).
8. Commission re higher education in West Indies, [Cmd.6654], *Parl.Pap.* 5 (1944—45): 791, at 44.
9. "Inter-University Council for Higher Education Overseas, 1946—54", [Cmd. 9515], *Parl.Pap.* 14 (1955—56): 843.
10. For developments in later 1950s, 1960s, see continuing series, "Report of the Commonwealth Education Conference", *Parl.Pap.* since 1958—59; also, "The Colonial Territories, 1958—59", [Cmd.780], *Parl.Pap.* 10 (1958—59): 475, at xxii, 112 ff.
11. On 1970s, scholarships, etc., see *Survey of Current Affairs* (annual), for example 3 (1973): 312, and (annual) *Yearbook of Commonwealth*; also, Ministry of Overseas Development, *Education in Developing Countries* (London: HMSO, 1970).
12. "Report of the Commission on Higher Education in the Colonies", [Cmd.6647] *Parl.Pap.* 4 (1944—45): 673, at 8, 104—13.
13. "Report of the Committee on Legal Education for Students from Africa", [Cmd.1255], *Parl.Pap.* 18 (1960—61): 719, at 4—6.
14. "Report of the West India Royal Commission", [Cmd.6607], *Parl.Pap.* 6 (1944—45): 245, at 135—55, 434.
15. See "The Colonial Empire (1939—47)", [Cmd.7167], *Parl.Pap.* 10 (1946—47): 403, at 13, 62—66; "Report on the Colonial Empire (1947—48)", [Cmd.7433], *Parl.Pap.* 11 (1947—48): 47, at 7, 49; "British Dependencies in the Far East, 1945—49", [Cmd.7709], *Parl.Pap.* 13 (1948—49): 371; "The Colonial Territories, 1958—59", [Cmd.780], *Parl.Pap.* 10 (1958—59): 475, at 139—41.
16. "Commonwealth Medical Conference, 1965", [Cmd.2867], *Parl.Pap.* 12 (1965—66): 25, at 4, 17: and second conference, [Cmd.3852], *Parl.Pap.* 28 (1968—69): 117, at 122.

20
An Evaluation

Possibly it is in cultural terms that decolonization of the empire has succeeded most, and perhaps with more success among the new members of the commonwealth than the old. In the latter case, the fact of the bulk of the population being of British stock has created some confusion as to cultural identity. There is, however, amongst all the commonwealth members one strong, continuing cultural bond centring on Britain — the use of the English language. In the eighteenth century the number of English speakers was smaller than speakers of French, Latin, German, Spanish, Russian and Italian. By the twentieth century English had a wider geographical range than any other tongue and it had become probably the most widely spoken language on earth; Chinese speakers were perhaps more numerous, but highly concentrated. It was estimated in the 1960s that about three hundred million people spoke English as their primary language while about six hundred million could use and understand it to some degree. In only one area, South Africa, has English declined quantitatively and been replaced as the major language.

English has become a universal language, in commerce, diplomacy, science, aviation, sport and scholarship. In many developing countries people prefer to learn English as their second language rather than the language of a neighbouring country. The dominance of the United States and wide dissemination through press and cinema have helped ensure the spread of the English language even though British power has been on the decline. In language, then, it may be argued that British cultural imperialism still reigns, but certainly not in an aggressive mood and with less concern for purity, or even dissemination, than in the case of the French language. Although bodies such as the British Council and the English Language Books Society have been concerned to help the use of English in developing countries it has not been accompanied by a sense of cultural aggression. Within the commonwealth, English has had to share the stage with a variety of languages: Hindi and other Indian languages, Chinese, Swahili, the wide range of African languages, Malayan, French, Dutch, Spanish and so on. But English has often proven to be the bond linking the different language groups. Papua New Guinea today in the confusion of hundreds of dialects looks to Pidgin English as a unifying bond.

The spirit of equality that pervades the present commonwealth has been aided partly by the improved nature of communications since 1945. The world of wireless and submarine telegraph cables has given way to more instant communication — submarine telephone cables and satellites. This has allowed all countries to make decisions immediately on matters that concern them. The spread of air services since 1945 has also had the effect of not only reducing the isolation of third world countries but also of building up their prestige and developing their independent status. After the war a flock of colonial airlines appeared, such as Megapode Airways in the British Solomons. In a number of cases the cost of such prestige was too high so that by the 1960s much rationalization had taken place, leading to the establishment of state flag-carriers. But all such developments in communications had the effect of helping to establish the independence and equal status of the new nations. The earlier notion of the empire as one world body offering the British example as the ideal towards which all other (and lesser) peoples should aim has been replaced by a group of independent nations, each asserting their own cultural identity but linked by a number of international influences, one of which is the commonwealth and another the English language. In effect, the commonwealth has become important as a means of communication.

Where the process of British decolonization has failed most is probably in the economic setting. Political preparation for independence did not proceed as thoroughly as the planners had hoped; but even with the rushed transfer of power it seemed in the long run that political control resting with popular local leaders rather than paternalistic foreign administrators would produce benefits for the whole of the community. Rushed economic development, however, could not so easily be effected and was more likely to lead to negative results for the community. In any case, while official policy set its course upon the transfer of political power to local hands neither the British government nor, more assuredly, the interests of world capitalism, contemplated the breakdown of metropolitan economic power and full devolution to local capitalists (or even socialists).

So the members of the commonwealth, old as well as new, have found themselves able to assert less economic independence than political. Certainly the colonial connections provided trading outlets, initiatives for modernization and some economic diversity for the colonies. But serious negative effects also occurred. Tropical colonies often found that the modernizing influences reduced local food production and otherwise distorted natural aspects of the economy. Too frequently when economic development was planned it was without sufficient knowledge of local conditions.

Imperial economic philosophy always emphasized the importance of colonies as areas of primary production to supply raw materials to the industrialized metropolitan power. Whenever crises of world capitalism occurred the primary producers were badly hit; in the twentieth century this problem was compounded by the ability of the industrial countries to fix prices more to their own advantage. Yet it was not invariably the case that a primary producing country was held back in economic development — for example, Australia rode ahead on many agricultural and mineral booms in the nineteenth century. At the same time the two most economically advanced members of the commonwealth, Canada and Australia, today have important economic weaknesses which stem partly from the colonial connection. In both cases they have relied heavily upon help from "big brother". By the mid-twentieth century Canada was very dependent upon mineral exports while her economy was dominated by United States finance. In 1964 sixty per cent of its total investment was held by foreigners, mainly from across the border. United States interests controlled sixty per cent of manufacturing, seventy-five per cent of petroleum and natural gas, sixty per cent of mining and smelting. Canada was dubbed as "the world's richest underdeveloped country" or "the world's most highly developed colony".

So the economic consequences of colonialism had mixed results, many of them negative. Industrialization was hindered but not prohibited. Development was slow but this did not necessarily mean that growth centres did not appear in the empire. For example, ideally placed entrepots such as Singapore and Hong Kong developed not only in trading strength but as financial and industrial centres. Today, however, the many weaknesses in the independent members of the commonwealth are not due solely to the British imperial heritage. Since 1945 development has become an unthinking end in itself; all countries embraced the vision of prosperity through the infusion of foreign capital. Today, economic distortions in a number of these countries are due more to the influence of American economic influence, operating through multinational corporations, than through British. Only in the 1970s has the illusion of unlimited growth and prosperity been revealed.

It was easy enough for Britain to give up political control over her empire, once she could no longer really hold it; it was easy enough for colonial peoples to assert equality and cultural identity, once their spirit of awareness had been aroused. The achievement of economic independence is a much more delicate affair. The economic relations of different countries are in continual flux; what is in balance today is out of balance tomorrow. The economies of empire countries have been significantly affected by the colonial connection; it is now the duty of the leaders of the commonwealth countries to work out some sort of balance of trade and finance between local needs and the international order. This has happened to some extent in the Lome convention where the EEC granted certain entry rights to Britain's former colonies in Africa, the Caribbean and the Pacific. Similar talks are going on with other trading bodies. At the same time leaders in these newly independent countries are now beginning to flex their economic muscle. Finding that the colonial experience entrenched the upper levels of economic power in overseas hands (generally from the metropolitan power), the leaders are now pushing policies of indigenization, and also acquisition of assets, so that the degree of foreign control is limited but generally not totally replaced. Mostly, policies of economic cooperation are being pursued.

In all, Britain's empire has not been the expected model of exploitation, violence or repression. Certainly there are individual examples of each of these ugly features of colonialism; sometimes there have been unwarranted excesses, mainly by British settlers rather than as a matter of official policy; but the overall picture has been one of moderation, balance and a high degree of passivity.

The time is at hand for the reassessment of the British imperial experience. Indian nationalists of the 1940s, and their African counterparts in the 1950s, might shrilly denounce the evils of British imperialism; but that propaganda war has now been won. Independence has been granted. The leaders of the new nations now drop the rhetoric of condemnation and instead seek cooperation. Although Marxist-Leninist prophecies might become fulfilled in the ruins of Portugal's African empire, the course of the British empire and the emergence of the commonwealth belie so many of those prophecies. Britain provided an example and a model of development, and although in many ways she bungled the execution of her imperial tasks, she did not ruthlessly impose her model. This left colonial areas free to adopt and adapt strands from the model, and increasingly to shape their own destiny. Colonial rule, by its very nature, meant some degree of imposition from above; obviously distortions of natural development did occur. Sometimes this imposed authority did offer a boost, and at other times it allowed considerable local initiative.

So, the consequences have not been all bad. It is time to evaluate the good along with the bad: it is time to sweep away the many prejudices, both for and against British colonialism, which have bedevilled the topic for many years. It is still too early to do a full balance-sheet of the benefits and disadvantages of British imperialism — if, indeed, it can ever be done. But it certainly is time for historians to make more soundly critical evaluations of topics like the following: the economic consequences flowing on from the imperial experience; the generation of world trade because of the imperial connection; the provision of schemes to develop the natural resources of the developing colonial countries; the construction of modern infrastructure — from roads to education — within traditional societies by the colonizing power; the health improvements, along with some disadvantages, that have flowed on from the imperial presence; the destruction of a traditional life — its politics, religion and way of life — and the consequence of westernization-modernization in areas reduced to a colonial role. This book makes a start in setting out an elementary framework out of which more detailed research and a more finite analysis can result.

From the end of the fifteenth century through to the latter part of the twentieth century British imperial power had turned almost a full circle, from little England to a free-ranging imperialism of free trade around the world, followed by the greatest colonial empire the world had ever known, and then a quick retraction back to Britain looking primarily towards involvement with Europe, just as in the fifteenth century. Over those centuries British imperial influence and power had operated through its agents applying skilfully the rules of the current mode of thinking:

- using the precepts of mercantile power to build up a strong navy, to obtain strategic bases, to gather in more people, to build up firm trading networks, in all to increase British total power beyond that of European rivals;
- being the first to understand and devise the system of free trade imperialism so that British traders and investors could function throughout the whole world, whether possessed by the British crown or not — and again British total power knew no rival;
- having put together this greatest of all colonial empires, sometimes by force, sometimes by trickery, sometimes almost by chance and even somewhat unwillingly, then holding it together by a fairly light system of overrule, which did not cost too much or involve too much British effort, and which did not impose too heavy a burden or crushing a subjugation upon the dependent peoples;
- and, finally, when this massive power in its territorial, military and economic senses was slipping away, deciding fairly directly to accept the erosion, again without too much cost to or loss by Britain.

So the commonwealth has emerged, the power is now diffuse. This club of members, whose only real likeness is the common sharing of a former colonial status, functions in a loose but basically friendly manner, to discuss mutual problems upon the basis of this joint heritage. The commonwealth, in a sense, hardly exists in tangible form; its economic advantages are slight and easily replaceable; its unity of purpose and power is weakened by compromise between the opposing views; but it is a means of communicating based upon the fact that all have been ruled by Britain. The social, cultural bonds provide a means of understanding. Britain, in the development of imperial power, has nurtured an extended family.

Index

Africa, central, 59, 114-15, 133, 142, 144, 161-67
Africa, east, 114, 117, 133, 142-43, 147, 150, 167
Africa, South, 8, 28, 47-48, 58, 66, 79-80, 87, 100, 102, 110-17, 123-24, 130-31, 161-67, 178, 191-93
Africa, west, 29, 33, 50, 70-73, 79, 81, 111, 114, 140-41, 151, 167, 173
Africans, 19-21, 87-88. See also Racial attitudes
aid, 34, 140-42, 183-86. See also Development
air transport, 201
America, Latin, 60-63, 112-13, 116-17, 165
American colonies, 7, 15, 22-23, 25-27, 35
American War of Independence, 27
Australia, 9, 29, 36, 47, 50, 53, 57-58, 61, 65-66, 80, 87, 89, 109-17, 121, 123, 131, 161-67, 191, 193

Bacon, Francis, 9
Bantustans, 193. See also Africa, South
bases, naval, 8, 49, 144
Boers, 100-101, 129, 140. See also Africa, South
Borneo. See Malaysia
Burma, 50, 101

Cables, 49, 122
Cabot, John, 5, 19
Canada, 8, 13, 28, 36, 47, 53, 57-58, 61, 65-66, 79-80, 109-17, 121, 133, 161-67, 191-92, 202
Cape Colony. See Africa, South
Ceylon, 8, 38, 74, 109-10, 114-15, 117, 143, 146-47, 167, 172. See also India
Chamberlain, Joseph, 107, 128, 141
Child, Joseph, 10, 26
China, 38-39, 59, 74, 112

Colombo plan, 185
Commonwealth, 29, 123, 171-72, 178-79
companies, chartered, 12-13, 25, 115, 133, 144-45
Crown colonies, 25, 28-29, 70, 137
Cyprus, 137, 176

Davenant, Charles, 29
defence, 34-36, 48-51, 102-05, 140, 159, 191
development, 31-34, 64-67, 76, 148, 153, 183, 189. See also aid
Dominions, 123-24
Durham report, 47
Dutch empire, 8

education, 22-23, 79, 121, 150-51, 194-96
Egypt, 100, 160, 178
Elizabeth I, 3-7
English language, 200

Federation, 48, 172, 177
Fiji, 50-51, 75, 89, 135, 149, 177, 194. See also Pacific, south
foreign jurisdiction legislation, 70-71, 101
free trade, 36-37, 46, 56-60, 76, 91-92
French empire, 8, 12, 45

German power, 98, 101-02, 105
Ghana, 110-11, 117, 141, 143, 145-46, 150, 162-63, 173-74, 185, 187, 195. See also Africa, west
Gibraltar, 8, 176
Gilbert, Humphrey, 5-6
Gold Coast. See Ghana
Grey, Henry (Lord), 46, 86

Haggard, Rider, 129
Hakluyt, Richard, 6-7
health, 81-82, 149-50, 197-98

Hong Kong, 59, 70, 74, 114, 145, 148, 161-64, 176, 187, 202. *See also* China

Imperial preference, 107-08, 112, 168
indentured labour, 88-89. *See also* Indian labourers
India, 12, 15, 37-38, 50-51, 57-58, 61-62, 65, 73, 80, 86, 90, 109-14, 125-26, 137, 148, 161-67, 170-71, 185
Indian labourers, 88-89, 130, 143, 194. *See also* Indentured labour
Indians, American, 19, 87. *See also* Canada
indirect rule, 134
industrialization, 32, 73, 120, 148, 186-87, 202
investment, 12, 60-65, 75, 113-38, 145-46, 165-68, 186-88
Irish Free State, 124, 178

Jamaica, 7, 21, 174. *See also* West Indies
Japanese power, 102, 104, 124, 191
jingoism, 129

Kenya, 135-36, 162, 172, 185, 187-88. *See also* Africa, east
Kipling, Rudyard, 129

Lugard, Frederick (Lord), 134

Malawi. *See* Rhodesia
Malaysia, 38, 70-71, 109-11, 114, 117, 134, 145-46, 151, 159, 161-67, 172-73, 177-78, 184-85, 187, 194
Malta, 8, 136, 176, 184
Maoris, 87, 131, 136, 149, 192. *See also* New Zealand
mercantilism, 8, 12-16, 31-37
middle east, 146, 164, 176, 178, 187
migration, 9-10, 53, 121, 191
military costs. *See* Defence
missionaries, 82-86, 150
motives, imperial, 3-11, 50-52, 63, 71, 99-100
Mun, Thomas, 13

Natal. *See* Africa, South
Nationalism, 26-27, 120, 125, 136-37, 160, 170-76, 187-88, 192, 203
neo-colonialism, 187-88, 192, 202
Newfoundland, 6, 124. *See also* Canada

New Guinea, 101, 175, 187. *See also* Pacific, south
New Hebrides, 85, 175. *See also* Pacific, south
New Zealand, 48, 50-51, 58, 61, 66, 80, 87, 109-15, 117, 123, 131, 161-67, 191-92
Nigeria, 70, 110-11, 117, 133, 141, 144, 149-50, 161-64, 174, 177, 185, 194. *See also* Africa, west
Nyasaland. *See* Rhodesia

oil, 118, 146, 187
Orange Free State. *See* Africa, South

Pacific, south, 39, 50, 71, 74, 85, 101, 145, 175-76, 189
Pakistan. *See* India
penal colonies, 9, 29
planters, 21-23, 32
Pownall, Thomas, 29
press, 125, 137-38

racial attitudes, 18-23, 83-84, 86-90, 92, 130-31, 176-77, 180, 192-94. *See also* Africans, Indians, Maoris
railways, 62, 65, 121, 141, 143
raleigh, Walter, 5
religion, 5-6, 9, 82-85, 136. *See also* missionaries
representative government, 26-27, 69, 172-75
resident system, 71, 134
responsible government, 46-47, 91, 136
Rhodes, Cecil, 101
Rhodesia, Northern and Southern, 103, 114, 117, 136, 145, 147-48, 161-63, 178-79, 191, 194
roads, 143-44

Sarawak. *See* Malaysia
shipping, 13-14, 33, 59, 187
Sierra Leone, 83, 174. *See also* Africa, west
Singapore, 104, 148, 162-64, 187, 202
slavery, 6, 9, 20-22, 33, 83-84. *See also* indentured labour, racial attitudes
Smith, Adam, 36-37
Solomon Island, 175. *See also* Pacific, south
Spanish empire, 3-6, 8
Sri Lanka. *See* Ceylon
sugar, 32, 36

INDEX

Tangania, 188. *See also* Africa, east
telegraph, 49, 122
trade, 7, 12-16, 31, 37, 57-60, 72-73, 103, 108-12, 144-45, 160-64
Transvaal. *See* Africa, South
Trusteeship, 83, 134-35, 153

universities, 121, 151, 196, 198

Vanuata. *See* New Hebrides
Virginia, 3, 7, 19-20, 23, 25-26. *See also* American colonies

Wakefield, Edward Gibbon, 47, 53
West Indies, 7-8, 15, 21-23, 27-28, 32-33, 35-36, 57, 69-70, 88, 109-111, 114, 141, 147, 167, 174, 184-85, 195, 197
Westminster, Statute of, 123-24
World War I, 103-04, 123
World War II, 103-04

Zanzibar, 74. *See also* Africa, east
Zimbabwe. *See* Rhodesia